A DEVELOPMENTAL NETWORK APPROACH TO THERAPEUTIC FOSTER CARE

by Paul Fine

The quality of mercy is not strained.
It droppeth as a gentle rain from heaven
Upon the place beneath: It is twice blessed;
It blesseth him that gives and him that takes.

—William Shakespeare
The Merchant of Venice

Child Welfare League of America
Washington, DC

Child Welfare League of America, Inc.
440 First Street, NW, Suite 310,
Washington, DC 20001-2085

Current Printing (last digit)
10 9 8 7 6 5 4 3 2 1

Cover and text design by Paul Butler

Printed in the United States of America
ISBN # 0-87868-509-X

CONTENTS

PREFACE

Family foster care placement, by offering opportunities for new and corrective experience, is a powerful social intervention capable of altering the fundamental focus and subsequent direction of child and family development. In spite of its power to improve lives, poorly conceived foster care can be catastrophic to child and family alike. Yet experience indicates that thoughtful planning and skillful care by a network of expert foster parents and well-informed professionals can produce positive results.

This book presents an original, case-focused, network-oriented approach to therapeutic foster care for older children who suffer from complex biogenic and socially derived developmental disorders. Until its close, the work described was carried out over approximately two decades, in the same community, often with the same families; and despite profound and frequent changes in the mental health and child welfare systems, the approach appears to have been effective. Details from a careful follow-up study are contained in three chapters of this book, but the book is, in fact, about loving care in the midst of change.

ACKNOWLEDGMENTS

The author is indebted to the following individuals, without whose efforts this book could not have been completed: Marcia W. Blum M.S.W., Pamela R. Fain Ph.D., Robert Towsend Ph.D., and Susan Eustice; and to the Edna McConnell Clark Foundation. This book is dedicated to the memory of Ezra Kohn M.S.W., Ph.D.

1. THE SETTING AND HISTORY OF THE PROGRAM

The experiences with therapeutic foster care described in this book originated during America's War on Poverty in the 1960s. It was widely believed at that time that the nation's rates of mental illness correlated with a vicious cycle of poverty, discrimination, and faulty child-rearing, and that these rates could be substantially reduced if certain social and environmental conditions were improved. As a consequence, residential treatment diminished, hospitals emptied, and community mental health centers were established throughout the country. Novel programs to improve child-rearing were well supported during the early years of the community mental health movement, and therapeutic foster care formed a part of these programs.

National policies were reflected locally in Omaha, Nebraska, by a broad-based citywide committee that convened in 1966 to establish mental health priorities for the area. Solutions did not come easily for this committee. In fact, it was only after five years of study and debate that consensus emerged. Of the committee's resultant priorities, the first was mental health services for children, and the second, specialized foster care. On the basis of these recommendations and a promise of federal support, an umbrella mental health agency was created for the region, and in 1972 the county sponsored a modest children's mental health program.

The program's mandate was to provide services for socially and economically disadvantaged children from dysfunctional families. On the basis of ecological notions concerning the impact of environmental variables on child and adolescent development and psychopathology [Auerswald 1968; Fine 1972; Hetznecker and Forman 1974; Malone et al. 1967; Minuchin et al. 1967; Speck and Attneave, 1973; Taber 1970],

1

therapeutic foster care was formulated as the linchpin for a comprehensive, accessible, and clinically effective children's program [Christensen and Fine 1979; Levin et al. 1976; Reiger 1972]. In a beehive of energy and idealism, a professional therapeutic foster care team was recruited, trained, and integrated with a small outpatient clinic, an educationally oriented day program, group homes, and contractual inpatient psychiatric services. Special attention was given to recruiting competent foster parents from a large pool of applicants and training them extensively in therapeutic foster care. Foster parents and children were patiently and carefully matched, and placement was made only after a comprehensive plan had been formulated for each situation. To help foster parents maintain and coordinate services for children who were placed, additional assistance was provided in the form of a support group in which caseworkers from the program and a consulting child psychiatrist participated regularly.

Looking back over those early years, it seems that local conditions were unusually receptive to therapeutic foster care. Administration was supportive, psychiatric and other technical services were easily accessible, and excellent foster homes were readily available. This ideal situation was short-lived, however. Mental health priorities soon changed nationally as well as locally, and support for integrated therapeutic foster care became increasingly problematic. For example, in 1975, the county authorities obtained a multimillion-dollar federal grant that mandated varied and widespread services for adolescents. The emphasis was on substance abuse. The regional agency expanded and its emphasis shifted from services for chronically disturbed children to acute care for adolescents. Consequently, the foster care team became less integrated with the agency, therapy for children in placement less well coordinated, and requests for therapeutic foster care increasingly nonspecific.

National developments in social welfare during the 1970s also compounded problems for therapeutic foster care in the mental health system. Widespread, documented abuses of custodial foster care grew into a national scandal [Fanshel and Shinn 1978; Goldstein et al. 1973; Gruber 1978; Knitzer 1978;

National Commission on Children in Need of Parents 1979; Swire and Kavaler 1977]. All foster care was called into question, and few efforts were made to emphasize the clear distinction between custodial and therapeutic models. In 1980 federal legislation was enacted to encourage states to improve conditions in foster homes, avoid unnecessary placements, maintain biological family unity, and support adoptions [Cox and Cox 1985]. Upon superficial application of these laws, a tendency emerged to view all foster care, including potentially therapeutic foster care, as part of a societal problem rather than as a valuable resource for psychiatrically disordered children and their families. Therapeutic foster care thus became identified with social welfare reform rather than mental health technique, and therapeutic programs were placed under the auspices of welfare rather than mental health agencies. As a result, interdisciplinary teamwork and psychiatric participation became the exception rather than the rule.

Locally, the federal seed grant for children's mental health services had expired, and because county funds were transferred to programs for chronically mentally ill adults, the therapeutic foster care program appeared to have run its course. At this juncture, to our delight and surprise, it was the foster parents who reaffirmed the program and demanded continuation. Positively impressed with the results, they were determined to follow through with the young people in their homes. Creighton University recognized that this particular group of parents was extraordinary and applied for private foundation support. The foundation, in turn, perceived promise in the local situation and granted financial aid in 1982.

The terms of the grant specified documentation, publication of results, and efforts to find the therapeutic program a permanent place in the overall care system. The grant was generous and welcome. Nevertheless, its immediate impact was destabilizing. Paradoxically, the grant tended to refocus the program toward nonclinical tasks such as accounting, recording, research procedures, and applications for new funding, sometimes at the expense of the time and energy necessary for effective clinical work [Fine and Taylor 1972]. Also, as the grant became known in

3

the community and attendant consultative relationships with local agencies were established, large—sometimes overwhelming—numbers of displaced, disturbed adolescents and children were referred to the University Clinic.

Moreover, in the face of complex additional demands, we could not find agency support to replicate the innovative, intrinsically well-coordinated clinical infrastructure of the program's earlier years. Thus, while important advances were being made in psychiatry, family therapy, and child protection, it remained difficult to incorporate the new techniques and new possibilities into the existing clinical system of therapeutic foster care. The progress in the field of child and adolescent psychiatry that could have been advantageously applied to therapeutic foster care over the years included an enhanced understanding of stress-related psychiatric disorders among abused and neglected children [Eth and Pynoos 1985; Terr 1991; Van der Kolk et al. 1985], improved diagnostic categories and measures [Achenbach and Edelbrock 1987; American Psychiatric Association 1987; Brandenberg et al. 1990], and specific indications for psychopharmacological intervention [Campbell and Spencer 1988].

Parallel advances in child welfare were also applicable, such as improved procedures for protecting children from neglect and abuse [National Association of Public Welfare Administrators 1988], special adoption programs [Cole 1985; Hill and Triseliotis 1991], and clinical techniques for family reunification [Bousha and Twentyman 1984; Bribitzer and Verdieck 1988]. In addition, applications of systems theory and family therapy increased in both fields [McGoldrick et al. 1982; Combrink-Graham 1990; Maluccio and Sinanoglu 1981], and although their practical incorporation into child and adolescent development, psychiatry, and other clinical disciplines would have been the logical next step, that step could not be taken. Public policy emphasized quick solutions, litigious approaches, and administrative methodologies which, even when unrealistic or ineffective, continued to be applied [Carbino 1991; Fine and Pape 1990].

Although by 1984 we had achieved some of the goals mandated by the grant, the pressures of clinical need eventually confronted us with a Hobson's choice: decrease funding-related activities or compromise clinical effectiveness. A formal study of the first eight years of operation had been accomplished, the foster parent support group had been preserved, and the clinical program had been kept alive, albeit in less than ideal form. It seemed clear that the grant had served a constructive purpose, but we also knew that the heart of our work was actual care for displaced, discarded, disrupted young people and their families through the application of clinically effective techniques. To preserve clinical integrity, it became necessary to concentrate our limited time and energy on direct, small-scale, high-quality services provided by a manageable clinical team of skilled foster parents, caseworkers, and a child psychiatrist. We therefore decided to persist in the refinement of our clinical techniques while awaiting more receptive times for their broader application.

In retrospect, our dilemma was not surprising. An imposing array of programmatic requirements and funding restrictions appears to have reflected an uninformed eagerness for immediate action in behalf of displaced children, a basic unwillingness to support expensive social programs, and a certain prejudice toward foster parents on the part of the public. Today, additional experience with the drawbacks of crisis-oriented methods has tempered the general enthusiasm for quick solutions and enabled the public to consider intensive clinical approaches, including therapeutic foster care [Fanshel et al. 1990; Hawkins and Breiling 1989; Meadowcroft and Trout 1991].

It has been over a generation since the beginnings of the community mental health movement, but only recently has the spirit of the times come into tune with our early experience in psychiatrically integrated, network-oriented foster care. Today, that work of the '60s is clearly seen as contemporary, necessary, and readily applicable to a wide variety of locations and systems.

REFERENCES

Achenbach, T.M., and Edelbrock, C.S. "Behavior Problems and Competencies Reported by Parents of Normal and Disturbed Children Aged 4 through 16." *Monographs of the Society for Research in Child Development* 46 (Serial #188), 1987.

American Psychiatric Association. *Diagnostic and Statistical Manual of Mental Disorders,* 3rd ed., Revised. Washington, DC: American Psychiatric Association, 1987.

Auerswald, E.H. "Interdisciplinary versus Ecological Approaches." *Family Process* 7, 2 (1968): 202-215.

Bousha, D.M., and Twentyman, C.T. "Mother-Child Interactional Style in Abuse, Neglect, and Control Groups: Naturalistic Observations in the Home." *Journal of Abnormal Psychology* 93, 1 (1984): 106-114.

Brandenberg, N.A.; Friedman, R.M.; and Silver, S.E. "The Epidemiology of Childhood Psychiatric Disorders: Prevalence Findings from Recent Studies." *Journal of the American Academy of Child and Adolescent Psychiatry* 29, 1 (1990): 77-83.

Bribitzer, M., and Verdieck, M.J. "Home-Based Family Centered Intervention: Evaluation of a Foster Care Prevention Program." *CHILD WELFARE* LXVII, 3 (1988): 255-266.

Campbell, M., and Spencer, E.K. "Psychopharmacology in Child and Adolescent Psychiatry: A Review of the Past Five Years." *Journal of the American Academy of Child and Adolescent Psychiatry* 27, 2 (1988): 269-279.

Carbino, Rosemarie. "Advocacy for Foster Families in the United States Facing Child Abuse Accusations: How Social Agencies and Foster Parent Organizations Are Responding to the Problem." *CHILD WELFARE* LXX, 2 (1991): 131-149.

Christensen, G., and Fine, P. "Corrective Socialization in Foster Care of Children." *Child Psychiatry and Human Development* 10, 1 (1979): 15-34.

Cole, E.S. "Adoption." In *Handbook of Child Welfare,* edited by J. Laird and A. Hartman. New York: The Free Press, 1985, 638-666.

Combrink-Graham, L. "Development in Family Systems Theory and Research." *Journal of the American Academy of Child and Adolescent Psychiatry* 29, 4 (1990): 501-512.

Cox, Martha J., and Cox, Roger, D. "A History of Policy for Neglected and Dependent Children." In *Foster Care: Current Issues, Policies, and Practices,* edited by Martha J. Cox and Roger D. Cox. Norwood, NJ: Ablex, 1985, 1-25.

Eth, S., and Pynoos, R.S. Post-Traumatic Stress Disorder in Children. Washington, DC: American Psychiatric Press, 1985.

Fanshel, D., and Shinn, E.B. *Children in Foster Care.* New York: Columbia University Press, 1978.

Fanshel, D.; Finch, S.J.; and Grundy, J.F. *Foster Children in a Life Course Perspective.* New York: Columbia University Press, 1990.

Fine, P. "An Appraisal of Child Psychiatry in a Community Health Project: Relevance as a Function of Social Context." *Journal of the American Academy of Child Psychiatry* 11, 2 (1972): 279-293.

Fine, P., and Pape, M. "Foster Families." In *Women's Progress: Promises and Problems,* edited by J. Spurlock and C. Rabinowitz. New York: Plenum Press, 1990, 35-58.

Fine, P., and Taylor, W.R. "Staff Supports; Lessons from the Child Guidance and Community Mental Health Movements." *Child Psychiatry and Human Development* 2, 1 (1972): 176-184.

Goldstein, J; Freud, A.; and Solnit, A.J. *Beyond the Best Interests of the Child.* New York: The Free Press, 1973.

Gruber, Alan R. *Children in Foster Care.* New York: Human Sciences Press, 1978.

Hawkins, R., and Breiling, J., eds. *Therapeutic Foster Care: Critical Issues.* Washington, DC: Child Welfare League of America, 1989.

Hetznecker, W., and Forman, M.A. *On Behalf of Children.* New York: Grune and Stratton, 1974.

Hill, M., and Triseliotis, J. "Subsidized Adoption across the Atlantic." *CHILD WELFARE LXX,* 3 (1991): 383-395.

Knitzer, Jane. *Children without Homes: An Examination of Public Responsibility to Children in Out-of-Home Care: Final Report.* Washington, DC: Children's Defense Fund, 1978.

Levin, S.; Rubenstein, J.S.; and Steiner, D.L. "The Parent Therapist Program: An Innovative Approach to Treating Emotionally Disturbed Children." *Hospital and Community Psychiatry* 27, 6 (June 1976): 407-410.

Malone, C.A.; Pavenstedt, E.; Mattick, I.; Bandler, L.S.; Stein, M.; and Mintz, N.L. *The Drifters: Children of Disorganized Lower Class Families.* New York: Little Brown, 1967.

Maluccio, A., and Sinanoglu, P. *The Challenge of Partnership: Working with Parents of Children in Foster Care.* New York: Child Welfare League of America, 1981.

McGoldrick, M.; Pearce, J.K.; and Giordano, J. *Ethnicity and Family Therapy.* New York: Guilford Press, 1982.

Meadowcroft, P., and Trout, B. *Troubled Youth in Treatment Homes: A Handbook of Therapeutic Foster Care.* Washington, DC: Child Welfare League of America, 1991.

Minuchin, S.; Montalvo, B.; Guerney, B.G., Jr.; Rossman, B.; and Schumer, F. *Families of the Slums: An Exploration of Their Structure.* New York: Basic Books, 1967.

National Association of Public Welfare Administrators. *Guidelines for a Model System of Protective Services for Abused and Neglected Children.* Washington, DC: American Public Welfare Association, 1988.

National Commission on Children in Need of Parents. *Who Knows? Who Cares? Forgotten Children in Foster Care.* New York: Institute of Public Affairs, 1979.

Reiger, N.R. "Changing Concepts in Treating Children in a State Mental Hospital." *International Journal of Child Psychotherapy* 1, 4 (1972): 89-116.

Speck, R.V., and Attneave, C. *Family Networks.* New York: Pantheon Books, 1973.

Swire, Margaret R., and Kavaler, Florence. "The Health Status of Foster Children." *CHILD WELFARE* LVI, 10 (1977): 635-653.

Taber, R.H. "A Systems Approach to the Delivery of Mental Health Services in Black Ghettos." *American Journal of Orthopsychiatry* 40, 3 (July 1970): 702-709.

Terr, L.C. "Childhood Traumas, An Outline and Overview." *American Journal of Psychiatry* 148, 1 (Jan. 1991): 10-20.

Van der Kolk, B.A.; Greenberg, M.; and Boyd, H. "Inescapable Shock, Neurotransmitters, and Addiction to Trauma: Toward a Psychobiology of Posttraumatic Stress." *Biological Psychiatry* 20, 3 (March 1985): 314-325.

2. CLINICAL PRINCIPLES AND PRIORITIES

The main therapeutic goal of foster care within our program was to help foster children construct adequate competence and a positive sense of self. Developmentally oriented and designed for relatively long-term applications, it provided ongoing parental relationships within which helpful, corrective, or compensatory social and emotional experiences could occur. Foster and adoptive parents were the primary therapists for this particular type of treatment, and their role was acknowledged as essential for its success. Accordingly, the program was designed to a large extent to support their efforts. Yet in order to be adequately therapeutic, the model had to meet other developmental needs as well, including those beyond family life and good parenting. The program was structured around three fundamental principles and six basic priorities to ensure that adequate consideration was given to all developmental needs in every case.

The basic principles underlying our approach to therapeutic foster care were and are the following:

- The individual in placement requires specific attention to his or her unique developmental needs;
- The foster family must remain functional for adequate care to be provided; and
- Social network principles apply, because foster children relate to more than one family.

Clinical priorities based on these three principles take practical considerations into account in the course of all decisions, large and small. In their usual order of importance, these priorities are:

- A safe and functional place to live,
- The provision of effective parenting,
- Opportunities for corrective emotional experience,

- Emotional continuity of significant love relationships, including those with biological relatives,
- Therapy for special needs, and
- Practical plans for permanency.

Basic Principles

As illustrated in figure 1, the basic principles of therapeutic foster care correspond to the individual, familial, and societal levels of the social system, and have functional implications for all work within the program.

Principle	Functional Implications
▪ Individual development	▪ Unique personal needs
▪ Family preservation	▪ Programmatic reinforcement
▪ Network support	▪ Social integration

Figure 1. System Principles Underlying the Therapeutic Foster Care Program

Individual Development. Because primary indications for therapy within this model involve distortions and disruptions of individual development, a clear and constant focus on developmental issues is basic to therapeutic foster care. In the model known today as continuous construction, development is defined as a complex process of dynamic transactions between an individual and his or her environment through which adaptational abilities are increased and elaborated. Normally, development is characterized by pattern continuity and punctuated by discontinuous biobehavioral shifts. Neurobiological, affectional, cognitive, and social factors are all involved in this developmental process. Although most elements of developmental discontinuity are genetically programmed, pattern continuity is essentially determined by the environment, which in turn depends largely on the stability of the family and the quality of parenting received [Zeanah et al. 1989]. Careful attention to patterns of continuity and discontinuity and an effective holding environment are essential for youngsters to benefit and progress in therapeutic foster care, because they must accept new homes, mourn losses, and become reinvolved with normal living patterns [Fein et al. 1990].

Foster children require supportive psychotherapy so that they may, in developmental terms, maintain constructive pattern continuity. Foster families have certain distinct advantages in this regard, the most obvious being that a well-functioning family is a normalizing environment for a child. Resilient foster families can provide structure for love and care and avoid further insults to normal development even under adverse conditions. In addition, good foster homes offer a vulnerable child new opportunities for close personal relationships with another set of parents and siblings, and guidance to apply the competencies thus acquired with neighbors, schoolmates, and members of his or her original family. Ideally, foster parents can then relate to and assist members of the child's original family on a basis of cultural parity. Finally, stable families are uniquely able to support and encourage foster children and their biological families long after placements have ended. After all, families have been the principal social institution for transmitting interpersonal traditions and relationships throughout the generations.

It is also true that discontinuous placement may present opportunities for reconstructive therapy and development toward more competent patterns, as described by Garmezy [1986] and Luthar and Zigler [1991]. The experience of change can, with expert guidance, enable the foster child to alter maladaptive patterns, acquire new social competencies, and heal old wounds. Nevertheless, psychotherapy that focuses on changing behaviors basic to the personality is usually painful and typically resisted, despite the fact that change may be perceived by the child as beneficial. It is for this reason that even the most experienced foster parents will require consultation for timing and technique in order to facilitate the developmental progress of the child in their care.

Family Preservation. Residential therapy within a family setting is not without liabilities. Some of the same sensitive and giving qualities that enable foster families to reach disturbed children and their relatives can make them vulnerable to both. Unlike staff members in other residential programs, foster parents can never completely escape their children's problems. Family morale may be challenged by a disturbed child's anxiety, misery, aggression, and stereotyped sexual behaviors, and the foster family's structure undermined by new premises and traditions from the child's family of origin. Thus, attention to conditions that protect and empower foster families was the second major principle underlying the program.

We took a functional approach to foster family support by selecting foster families for attributes of strength and stability and helping them cope on their own terms. The philosophy inherent in this approach, in which human nature, cultural traditions, and basic individual needs are central to each person's well-being, has recently been termed *postmodernism* [Murphy and Callaghan 1989]. Guidelines for staff support based on this philosophy derived from four requisites of small-group functioning: commitment to the group by its members, consensus about norms within the group, control of resources by the group, and secure boundaries with concomitant flexibility that permits openness to individuals and systems outside the group [Tallman 1971]. Mutual commitments between youngsters being placed and their foster families were facilitated by careful matching, preplacement visits, and gradual integration. Ongoing consensus within the foster family was supported by respite care or extra staff support when necessary and regular visits from a program caseworker. Total resource control by the foster family was reinforced by adequate financial reimbursement and support for family decisions concerning allocation of these resources. Boundary flexibility was promoted by frequent meetings of a foster parent support group around shared concerns and by clear administrative support.

It was understood that placement of a young person away from the family of origin was also bound to affect that family profoundly in terms of ongoing commitments, consensus, resource control, and openness to others. To some extent, therefore, the same requisites of small-group functioning were also applied by the staff in working with foster children's biological families. Unlike the therapeutic families, however, who were characterized by strength and stability, biological families were frequently in need of multiple social, medical, and mental health services. Advocacy and coordination with other agencies that were providing services to the foster children's original families thus became a function of the program's concern for adequate care. The challenge was to maintain the family of origin rather than to restructure it by permanently excluding the offspring who had been placed in family foster care.

Network Support. Systematic reliance on social networks was the third major element underlying the program. This proved to be a useful method for resolving some of the complexities thus far discussed. Networks—defined as the personal matrices of relationships that interconnect individuals, families, and other groups within a community—are intrinsic to foster care, and can be used to broaden families' social orientation as well as achieve complex therapeutic goals [Fine 1973]. Although this inclusive approach was at times administratively inconvenient, its results usually justified the extra effort.

While network applications pervaded the program, they were used in at least six specific and interrelated ways: (1) to help the foster child avoid or resolve loyalty conflicts; (2) to help the child and the family of origin establish additional positive relationships; (3) to provide a consistent means of support and mutual aid for foster families; (4) to establish links within the professional community; (5) to enhance a particular form of family system therapy; and (6) to ensure ongoing support after a child left the program.

We knew that the foster children in our program could benefit if they became close to the therapeutic foster family, but we also knew that conflicting loyalties could keep them from achieving closeness. Our solution to this paradox was to help the foster children establish familylike relationships with members of the foster family, while at the same time preserving equivalent relationships within the family of origin. In this way, an inclusive network of family members and other caring adults was established to facilitate positive long-term development. Openness, diplomacy, patience, sensitivity, accurate timing, persistence, and a good deal of effort were usually required before parallel relationships of this type could become functional. Moreover, the approach was effective only when the foster child's family of origin was neither dangerous nor overtly rejecting.

Generally, the fact that the biological family shares a child in common with the foster family can create a rich variety of relationships, some of which can be uncommonly positive. For example, one foster mother in our program helped the mother of her foster son care for her new baby and suggested ways to cope with details of the welfare system. In another instance, a foster parent invited the older brother of his foster son to join the Boy Scout troop he led. In both situations, supportive familylike relationships between the child's foster and original families were established. Many similar relationships persisted with a measure of success even after the children had left the program.

Network concepts were also applied toward direct support of the foster families. As discussed in chapter 6, most foster parents who worked with the program maintained extensive personal networks of friends, relatives, and professional contacts. Encouraging foster parents to use their existing networks was an important feature of the program. In addition, the foster parent support group provided a matrix for networking among foster families within the program. Over time, foster families helped each other with baby-sitting, respite care, and crisis resolution, and an extensive list of resources was constructed from their combined knowledge about the community. Day care workers, special education teachers, attorneys, social workers, psychologists, psychiatrists, and other helping professionals were all frankly discussed by the group in relation to particular problems within the context of the therapeutic program.

It was not unusual for the children in our program, along with their families, to continue in the numerous personal and professional relationships that had originated during previous placements. Occasionally, these relationships added an element of confusion to their lives. Although standard professional approaches to collaboration were usually sufficient to clarify and reorganize situations of this type, it was sometimes necessary to apply more formal network techniques [Rueveni 1979; Speck and Attneave 1973]. For example, the biological mother of one of the children in placement was meeting regularly with a variety of teachers, welfare caseworkers, psychotherapists, and a previous foster parent, but did not incorporate the current therapeutic foster mother into these discussions. A network meeting was carefully arranged with the mother, her older sister, the previous foster parents, the current foster mother, and four case-related professionals, which led to a more beneficially organized program. In another instance, the staff helped an isolated, chronically depressed single mother to meet with her son and his therapeutic foster family in a manner that led to a permanently supportive relationship.

Clinical Priorities

Six clinical priorities were developed to integrate the basic principles discussed above with other practical and administrative imperatives. These priorities were guidelines for day-to-day decisions within the program. Although figure 2 lists the six priorities in their general order of importance, all are considered essential and are meant to be applied with flexibility and common sense.

A Safe and Functional Home. Security and protection are fundamental to normal childhood development, and are necessary prerequisites for successful therapy. Basic security for any child includes the adequate provision of food, shelter, health maintenance, and physical safety within a functional home. Safety for the child was always given first priority in our program, but it was approached in a manner that also provided security for the foster family. For example, children who had experienced abuse tended to expect further abuse and acted out

Priority	Rationale
▪ A safe and functional home	▪ Basic security and protection
▪ Effective parenting	▪ Competent development
▪ Relationship therapy	▪ Corrective experiences
▪ Continuity with loved ones	▪ Identity and self-esteem
▪ Specific therapy for special needs	▪ Comprehensive treatment
▪ A plan for family permanency	▪ A secure future

Figure 2. Clinical Priorities for Care within the Therapeutic Foster Care Program

their feelings and fears in a number of provocative behaviors. These behaviors included gorging vast quantities of food, hiding feces around the home, sexual provocation, blatant aggression, stealing followed by overt denial, and complex and unfounded negative fantasies about the foster family. One boy burned down the foster home soon after his arrival. Yet, remarkably, the foster family assumed full financial responsibility and the placement was preserved. Children with such extreme behaviors had typically experienced emotional trauma within previous unsuccessful placements and had often been removed from these placements for their own protection. Some had suffered further abuse by biological relatives during visits or attempts at reunification, and for most, problems had been compounded by sudden and unexpected changes from home to home.

Therapeutic foster homes in our program came under close scrutiny for safety and security during licensing. Continual working relationships with the staff during weekly visits to these homes maintained the focus on safety. Occasionally, foster parents were accused of abuse or neglect by foster children or their biological families. Yet such accusations were seldom serious, and none resulted in criminal prosecution or removal of a child from the foster home. The task in these instances was to investigate the complaint in a dignified manner, protect the child and the foster family from hair-trigger responses, and survive the episode with minimal damage to everyone involved. It was always a major challenge for the staff to attend to child protection and security while not becoming triangulated against the foster parents or the child in a manner that could paralyze other essential elements of care. In most instances, the staff was able to intervene preventively when required, maintain constructive relationships with appropriate state agencies, and preserve a healing atmosphere for both the child and the foster home.

Effective Parenting. Effective, predictable parenting is the second indispensable prerequisite for therapy within a foster home, and was the second clinical priority for day-to-day decisions within the program. In a practical sense, this requisite is an acknowledgment that running a household and raising children, which are normally manifold and time-consuming tasks, can become extraordinarily complex in the case of foster care.

Essentially, the parenting relationship helps to create an emotional climate within which wholesome child development can proceed. Elements that contribute to effective parenting in the foster home include an attitude toward the child of positive regard, affection, consistency, and accurate empathy [Truax and Carkhoff 1967]. Parental tasks vary with the age of the child. For example, although age-appropriate concerns center around the home, for toddlers, they expand to include the school and neighborhood during middle childhood, and the world at large during adolescence.

Many of the children in our program required inordinate attention for even the simplest daily routines. Getting up, toileting, washing, dressing, meals and manners, going to school and staying there, playing, quiet time, and going to bed typically required extra care. Minor illnesses and injuries called for special comforting. Similarly, appropriate behavior around holidays and developmental milestones could rarely be taken for granted. Milestone events, such as weaning, toilet training, birthdays, entering kindergarten, puberty, confirmation, dating, and getting a first job, tended to be overstimulating for most of the children.

Careful monitoring, thoughtful timing, and staff support for the foster parents were essential to prevent some types of events from impeding normal parenting. For example, contacts with members of the biological family, therapeutic confrontations within the foster home, court procedures, agency reviews, and elective medical procedures could all become necessary from time to time, and had to be managed in ways that would interfere least with normal development. The child's degree of incorporation into the foster home was always a major consideration in this regard.

Corrective Experience. Corrective emotional experience through relationship therapy in a family milieu was a central priority for our program, and was taken into account during all clinical decisions. The basic premise for this therapy was that each child could acquire improved social and emotional competencies by incorporation into, and differentiation from, the foster family. The process resembled, but went a step beyond, normal parenting. In addition, it was complementary to other forms of therapy the child might require, rather than a substitute for them.

Target symptoms for relationship therapy were identified by observing certain behavioral patterns, and formulated simultaneously in terms of developmental pathology. Three patterns were identified and measured for signs of improvement over time: conservation-withdrawal, protest-attention demanding, and stereotyped repetitive patterns of family triangulation. The concept of conservation-withdrawal is formulated as a response to loss and associated with depression, psychosocial growth retardation, pain insensitivity, and other physiological problems [Engel 1962; Goldfarb 1945; Kaufman 1991; Money et al. 1983]. Protest-attention demanding is conceptualized in terms of the fight or flight responses of aggression, hyperactivity, and anxiety [George and Main 1979; Seay et al. 1962; Weininger 1972]. The repetitive pattern of triangulation is thought to represent maladaptive internalized patterns of basic relationships [Green and Gaines 1984; Kluft 1985; Littner 1975]. These three patterns of developmental pathology are understood to alternate and interact with each other, and in order to study them, we devised the rough, empirically derived scale described in chapter 4.

Therapy itself was conceptualized in Piagetian terms, as part of the developmental process by which a child could accommodate to the foster home and thus assimilate more competent patterns of adaptation [Decarie 1965]. Stages for therapy were also formulated according to Piaget, as engaging with the foster parents and the new environment, becoming attuned to the new environment, coordinating personal routines and emotional patterns within the relationship and the home, intentionally applying new behaviors, experimenting with fresh emotional and behavioral patterns, and insightfully applying new abilities.

We expected to see a rough correspondence of Piaget's stages to the progress of a child's relationship with foster parents, including initial bonding, attachment, constancy, individuation, relative emancipation, and mature dependency. Timing for these stages was anticipated in terms of weeks for the initial stage, moving to months, and then years for the final stage [Christensen and Fine 1979]. Caseworkers kept a record of each child's behavior within the home, which was later analyzed for evidence of improvement or regression in target areas. Although a certain unavoidable amount of resistance and emotional pain was expected during therapy, the staff focused on working through problems between the foster child and the foster parents in terms of the therapeutic goals to be attained.

Emotional Continuity. The next essential priority for children within the program was the protection of their sense of identity, self-esteem, and belonging by means of continuity with loved ones. In all cases, therefore, as much knowledge as possible was gathered concerning the child's family ties, and a plan was then formulated to reinforce positive relationships and work through those that were ambivalent. Timing and focus for this process were integrated with other requisites for therapy, since forced or poorly integrated contact was generally considered counterproductive.

In most instances, the child's loved ones were relatives, and continuity was encouraged through a series of gradually integrated contacts between the foster and biological families. The usual sequence was for the staff to review details with the foster parents, and then for foster parents to meet the biological parents and staff members in a neutral location or at the foster home. This was followed by family visits with the child in the foster home and, when possible, gradually extended visits at the biological family's home. Responses and reactions to visits could then be discussed and worked through by the child, biological family members, and foster parents. The overriding goal of contact was personal and family integration. A similar approach was applied when adoptive relatives, previous foster parents, or even staff members from institutional placements were significant to the child.

In a few cases, there was no knowledge or even memory of biological parents and minimal evidence of any family ties. Other children had been so abused that they expressed only negative feelings about their parents and clearly did not want contact with them. Yet even in these cases, positive memories and identifications could be sought and emotional acceptance and reconciliation encouraged. Occasionally, long-separated siblings were reunited in this way.

Therapy for Special Needs. The fifth essential priority for the children in our program was specific attention to special needs. These children typically suffered from a wide variety of self-reinforcing medical, dental, educational, psychiatric, and substance-related disorders and disabilities that required visits to a variety of specialists. The key here was for the staff to approach the list of special needs as economically as possible in terms of time and energy, and to plan for essential therapies in a way that did not overwhelm the child's security or undermine relationship therapy within the foster home.

Counseling relationships with the children were routinely established by the program's social workers. Necessary confidentiality, as defined by legal parameters, was preserved, but openness was encouraged whenever possible, and the foster parents were included in most sessions. Counseling for personal considerations, such as fearfulness, overdependency, and peer problems, could then be integrated with similar efforts on the part of foster parents, and in some instances led to network sessions that included other significant adults. Problems of a more intimate nature sometimes required confidentiality, but in all instances foster parents were dealt with openly and genuinely, as one would deal with any parent, and their consent and cooperation were actively sought.

Certain psychiatric disorders prevalent in this population required consultation or direct attention from a licensed mental health professional. For example, cognitive approaches might be applied for depression, confrontation for conduct disorders, rage-reduction for lack of attachment, catharsis for post-traumatic stress disorder, integrative approaches for dissociative states, tension reduction for anxiety, mourning for grief reactions, and reality testing for micropsychotic episodes. Psychopharmaco-therapy was also used when appropriate, as well as psychiatric hospitalization and special programs for survivors of incest and physical or substance abuse. Here, as in all situations throughout the program, great care was required to maintain relationship therapy within the foster home and continuity with other essential aspects of the child's treatment.

A final set of special needs arose from the fact that many of the children also suffered from learning disabilities and associated neurogenic problems, as described in chapter 4. Collaboration among staff members, foster parents, and special education personnel then became necessary to ensure that the child's needs for concrete structure, understandable language, and survival skills would be respected.

Plans for Permanency. Planning for permanent membership within a family was the sixth essential priority in the program and an element in all clinical decisions. The rationale behind this priority was that membership in a family would support the child's sense of identity, self-image, and inner security throughout the inevitable vicissitudes of life [Goldstein et al. 1973]. State and federal programs that now help agencies plan for permanent family arrangements were not prevalent at the time. As a consequence, this task fell directly upon the program staff. The preferred outcome for permanent placement, then as now, was for the child to return to an improved situation within his or her own family, and the staff always tried to work with, or find services for, families to encourage this outcome. Many of the children did, in fact, return to a strengthened family of origin.

In the event that a return to the original family was found to be impractical or dangerous, the next most desirable plan usually involved adoption. In these cases, the staff typically sought funding for adoption subsidies and medical coverage, negotiated arrangements that were open to contact with biological relatives, when appropriate, and provided other specific supports for adoption. As a result, a significant proportion of children were eventually adopted by foster parents associated with the program. A certain number of children, however, could not return to the biological family and would not accept adoption. These were usually individuals who maintained intensely ambivalent ties with abusive biological relatives and were unable to accept what they perceived as permanent rejection and defeat. Legal guardianship was occasionally arranged in lieu of adoption, but the usual plan for these cases was ongoing placement in an effort to construct a network of caring adults. Options for permanent security within a family were not always clearly evident on a day-to-day basis for many children within the program, and even a carefully crafted permanency plan could change as circumstances changed from year to year. Although family permanency was considered essential, patience was required to work with the entire situation pending clear resolution of the complexities that pervaded these children's lives.

REFERENCES

Christensen, G., and Fine, P. "Corrective Primary Socialization in Foster Care of Children." *Child Psychiatry and Human Development* 10, 3 (Fall 1979): 15-34.

Decarie, T. *Intelligence and Affectivity in Early Childhood.* New York: International University Press, 1965.

Engel, G.L. "Anxiety and Depression-Withdrawal: The Primary Affects of Unpleasure." *Index Medicus* 43 (March–June 1962): 89-97.

Fein, E.; Maluccio, A.N.; and Kluger, M. *No More Partings: An Examination of Foster Family Care.* Washington, DC: Child Welfare League of America, 1990.

Fine, P. "Family Networks and Child Psychiatry in a Community Health Project." *Journal of the American Academy of Child Psychiatry* 12, 4 (October1973): 675-689.

Garmezy, N. "Children under Severe Stress: Critique and Commentary." *Journal of the American Academy of Child and Adolescent Psychiatry* 25, 1986: 384-392.

George, C., and Main, M. "Social Interactions of Young Abused Children: Approach, Avoidance, and Aggression." *Child Development* 50, 2 (June 1979): 306-311.

Goldfarb, W. "Psychological Privation in Infancy and Subsequent Adjustment." *American Journal of Orthopsychiatry* 15, 3 (April 1945): 247-255.

Goldstein, J; Freud, A.; and Solnit, A.J. *Beyond the Best Interests of the Child.* New York: The Free Press, 1973.

Green, A.H., and Gaines, R. "Child Abuse: Pathological Syndrome of Family Interactions." *American Journal of Psychiatry* 131 (1984): 882.

Kaufman, J. "Depressive Disorders in Maltreated Children." *Journal of the American Academy of Child and Adolescent Psychiatry* 30, 2 (March 1991): 257-265.

Kluft, R. *Childhood Antecedents of Multiple Personality Disorder.* Washington, DC: American Psychiatric Association Press, 1985.

Littner, N. "The Importance of Natural Parents to the Child in Placement." *CHILD WELFARE* LIV, 3 (1975): 175.

Luthar, S., and Zigler, E. "Vulnerability and Competence: A Review of Research on Resilience in Childhood." *American Journal of Orthopsychiatry* 6, 1 (1991): 6-22.

Money, J.; Annecillo, C.; and Kelly, J.F. "Growth of Intelligence: Failure and Catch-Up Associated Respectively with Abuse and Rescue in the Syndrome of Abuse Dwarfism." *Psychoneuroendocrinology* 8, 3 (1983): 309-319.

Murphy, J., and Callaghan, K. "Therapeutic versus Traditional Foster Care: Theoretical and Practical Distinctions." *Adolescence* 24, 96 (1989): 891-900.

Rueveni, R. *Networking Families in Crisis.* New York: Human Sciences Press, 1979.

Seay, B.; Hansen, E.; and Harlow, H.F. "Mother-Infant Separation in Monkeys." *Journal of Child Psychology and Psychiatry* 3-4, 2 (1962): 123-132.

Speck, R.V., and Attneave, C. *Family Networks.* New York: Pantheon Books, 1973.

Tallman, I. "Family Problem Solving and Social Problems." In *Family Problem Solving,* edited by J. Aldous. Hinsdale, IL: Dryden Press, 1971, 257-270.

Truax, C., and Carkhoff, R. *Toward Effective Counseling and Psychotherapy.* Chicago: Aldine Publications, 1967.

Weininger, O. "Effects of Parental Deprivation: An Overview of Literature and Report on Some Current Research." *Psychological Reports* 30, 2 (April 1972): 591–612.

Zeanah, Charles H.; Anders, Thomas F.; Seifer, R.; and Stein, D.N. "Implications of Research in Infant Development for Psychodynamic Theory and Practice." *Journal of the American Academy of Child and Adolescent Psychiatry* 28 (April 17, 1989): 657-668.

3. ESSENTIALS OF THE TREATMENT TEAM

The principles of therapeutic foster care outlined in the previous chapter were systematically applied by a treatment team composed of foster parents, two full-time caseworkers, and one part-time child psychiatrist. The main function of this team was to join with a child's social/developmental network as a generally positive influence in his or her life. Members could then use their particular skills, with reciprocity, toward specific treatment goals. As a general rule, foster parents were focal for child and family development, while caseworkers maintained supportive services and the child psychiatrist provided mental health expertise.

In practice, each foster child's social/developmental network was extremely complex, usually involving members of at least two families, neighborhoods, and school systems. Because of this complexity, guidelines derived from sociological levels of network organization were useful in formulating the therapeutic process.

Levels of Network Interaction

The primary, secondary, and tertiary levels of network organization are illustrated in table 1. Primary groups and networks are close and intimate, and maintain frequent social contact [Cooley 1909]. Parenting, for example, typically occurs at the primary level, as do psychotherapeutic and other deeply emotional relationships. As outlined in chapter 2, a principal goal of the treatment team was to help foster children achieve close, constructive relationships with their foster parents for purposes of normal development and relationship therapy. Foster children also usually maintained their primary relationships with loved parents, close friends, and other personally important individuals.

Table 1. Levels of Network Organization for Children in Therapeutic Foster Care

Level	Defining Characteristics	Examples of Relevant Social Groups
Primary	▪ Dyads and small groups ▪ Close and intimate relationships ▪ Continuing frequent contact ▪ Concerned with personal matters	▪ Nuclear biological family ▪ Therapeutic foster family ▪ Psychotherapy group ▪ Close friends ▪ Study group within a classroom ▪ Worship group ▪ Physician-patient relationship
Secondary	▪ Intermediate-size groups ▪ Nonintensive relationships ▪ Continual but less frequent contact ▪ Concerned with mutual interests	▪ Extended biological family ▪ Extended foster family ▪ Neighborhood play group ▪ Self-help group ▪ School and classroom ▪ Church circle ▪ Medical clinic personnel
Tertiary	▪ Large groups ▪ Impersonal relationships ▪ Infrequent and discontinuous contact ▪ Concerned with economics and administration	▪ Formal family organization ▪ Sponsoring agency ▪ Case review board ▪ Welfare department ▪ School system ▪ Church organization ▪ Health maintenance organization

Secondary groups and networks are more casual and interact less regularly than primary groups. Normally, they are the level at which classrooms, clubs, play groups, and extended families function [Burgess 1929], and they provide direct links between the nuclear family and the outside world [Moncreif and Brassard 1979]. Because secondary relationships are usually determined for children by where they and their parents live, foster children typically require help in constructing new secondary relationships when placed in a foster home.

Tertiary groups and networks do not meet regularly, but come together as needed, usually over issues involving power and money. Children normally do not play a direct role in tertiary networks. However, because they are not protected by a permanent biological or adoptive family and may be wards of the state, foster children are unusually vulnerable to tertiary political and economic events.

Family Networks and the Treatment Team

In our program, the treatment team offered direct services on all network levels and coordinated outside assistance when necessary. Therapeutic plans for each child could thus be formulated in accordance with the principles and priorities discussed in chapter 2. First, each core team would join with the child, and his or her family when appropriate, to create and nurture surrogate networks and conduct the work of therapy. Core team meetings were held regularly to support these processes. Second, all foster parents and professional staff members met together once or twice a month for long hours in the evening to review cases, exchange opinions, and provide mutual support. These meetings, along with occasional picnics and get-togethers, became a true support network that lasted many years. Finally, administrative procedures were created and designed to be clear cut, positive, and as easy to accomplish as possible.

Table 2 illustrates therapeutic tasks that members of the core team could perform as functions of each network level. The role of each member is discussed below.

The Role of Foster Parents. An initial primary attachment by the foster child to a foster parent was considered critical to the facilitation of cognitive, social, and emotional development and therapy within the home and family. Functions of this therapeutic attachment are comparable to those of mothers with their small children, and include teaching the child adaptive techniques for closeness, clues to dangerous situations, and appropriate responses [Bretherton and Walters 1985; Stroufe 1988]. Competencies that

Table 2. Functions of Therapeutic Team

Network Level	Foster Parents
Primary	▪ Regular parenting ▪ Therapeutic parenting ▪ Support for biological parents ▪ Role model for biological parents
Secondary	▪ Provide connections in the school, neighborhood, social group, and faith community ▪ Access extended family resources ▪ Network with foster child's biological family
Tertiary	▪ Advocate within legal, welfare, and school systems ▪ Maintain formal relationship with sponsoring agency

derive from this initial attachment are first tied to the mother or another attachment figure, but subsequently become self-regulating and generalized within the primary social network [Fine 1973; Grossman and Grossman 1991].

Foster parents in our program also frequently established unique primary network relationships with the children's parents, siblings, and other relatives. The college-educated mother of one depressed foster child was ineffective at parenting, and her life was in turmoil due to lifelong borderline personality traits. She developed a close relationship with her daughter's foster mother and used this relationship for support during times of crisis. For example, she called on the foster mother to discuss elective surgical procedures, to help herself control overeating and drinking, and to forestall suicide gestures and attempts. Over the years, the relationship introduced an element of stability to her life and enabled her to share some of the values her

Members by Level of Network Organization

Program Caseworkers	Child Psychiatrist
▪ Counsel foster child ▪ Counsel biological family ▪ Casework and respite care ▪ Direct support to foster family	▪ Evaluate foster child ▪ Evaluate relatives ▪ Provide direct treatment as requested
▪ Maintain treatment continuity for child across placements ▪ Maintain professional referral network for social and family services, group homes, and rehabilitation services	▪ Serve as consultant for treatment process ▪ Maintain continuity with psychiatric resources ▪ Maintain professional referral network for related medical and hospital services
▪ Advocate for child, family, and foster family ▪ Maintain formal agency and placement requirements	▪ Advocate for children, families, and foster families ▪ Facilitate accreditation requirements and program advocacy

daughter acquired in the foster home. With this help, and a variety of psychiatric and psychotherapeutic treatments outside the program, she eventually achieved adequate functioning, both personally and as a parent.

By the same token, each foster parent's network of secondary relationships with neighbors, schools, churches,* sports organizations, and clubs was available to foster children, and sometimes led to helpful and lasting friendships for the children's biological families. In several instances, the biological family joined the foster parent's church. Even now, years later, one woman continues to attend church with her previous foster

*The word *church* will be used throughout this volume, instead of the more inclusive *religious community,* because in this particular group of foster parents, to the best of our knowledge, all were either Christian (the large majority) or professed no affiliation.

parents, who also frequently baby-sit the woman's children and are considered to be the grandparents of her family.

At times, foster parents would advocate for children and families with political and bureaucratic organizations. For example, to meet the special needs of her foster child, one foster parent was instrumental in creating a special junior high school program for children with developmental disabilities. Further, it was not unusual for foster parents to appear before courts and agencies on behalf of the children in their care. The team always supported these efforts.

The Role of the Caseworkers. There were usually two caseworkers on the treatment team. Their caseloads were small and manageable, administration was supportive, and close relationships with foster parents were well maintained. Specific tasks for the caseworkers on a primary level consisted of individual counseling with the foster children, support for the foster family, and direct work with the biological families. The following example illustrates how caseworkers functioned on this level:

> Two young sisters, both of whom suffered from cystic fibrosis, were placed in therapeutic foster care directly from the hospital, following a life-threatening crisis brought about because their parents, who were divorcing, had become demoralized and could not help them adhere to the special diet vital to their health. Their biological mother was clinically depressed and their father overanxious. Although both acted guilty and avoidant, neither parent would accept psychotherapeutic help. Nevertheless, both girls missed their parents and craved contact. The caseworker consequently established supportive relationships with each of the foster children, their biological mother and her parents, the biological father and later his new wife, and members of the foster family of six. Over the months, the caseworkers used these relationships to support the placement, counsel the girls and their parents, and enable all concerned to focus on treatment goals. It was largely due to the caseworker's efforts that both girls were able to live relatively normal and remarkably healthy lives. The foster parents soon felt free to discard the undertaker's business card that had been given them when the girls first came to their home.

Each caseworker also maintained a secondary network of practical resources in behalf of her or his clinical caseload. Resources that were frequently called upon included the local welfare office, child protective services, school systems, rehabilitation specialists, special services for the developmentally disabled, vocational rehabilitation services, programs for incest survivors, shelters, family service agencies, and a network of local psychotherapists, respite care providers, homemaking services, drug and alcohol programs, group homes, and residential facilities. For the caseworker to integrate these various services with ongoing professional and therapeutic relationships was a major task.

It was the caseworkers, more than anyone else, who held the program together. They were instrumental in licensing, arranging meetings both routine and extraordinary, and facilitating continuity in a manner that made the program more than the sum of its individual placements. It was not unusual for a caseworker to create a temporary, supportive, goal-oriented network of services and relationships when a placement was disrupted and the child went from a foster home to a group home, a hospital, or another family foster home placement. In these situations, the caseworker would attempt to heal relationships in the previous home, prepare for the next location, inform relatives, help the child salvage personal gains, and arrange necessary school and agency contracts.

The Role of the Child Psychiatrist. Our program was distinctive in that a child psychiatrist formed an integral part of the treatment team. As documented in chapter 4, psychopathology was frequent among the foster children and their biological families. Although direct diagnosis and therapy at the psychiatrist's office or in the hospital played an occasional role in the program, more frequently the psychiatrist functioned as a member of the team. Professional competencies essential for the psychiatrist in this context included general knowledge of the principles of child development, psychopathology, and therapeutic modalities. Frequently required were techniques to help children work through emotional separation and loss [Fein et al. 1990] and facilitate moral development [Kohlberg 1978], emotional adaptation [Ekstein 1966], family stability [Reiss 1981], parenting relationships [Scharff 1989], specific psycho-pharmacotherapy, health-related factors [Schor 1982], and special services within school systems, such as diagnosis of learning disabilities [Rae-Grant 1989]. Access by the psychiatrist to the entire network of mental health, psychiatric, and medical specialties added another dimension to the resources the team could make available in each case. It was from this vantage that the psychiatrist played a role in case planning, training staff members and foster parents, placing foster children in suitable homes, monitoring the treatment process, and providing technical advice during team and support-group meetings. When requested, the psychiatrist joined foster parents and caseworkers in meetings with welfare department personnel, school administrators, rehabilitation staff members, other physicians and therapists, and biological relatives. The psychiatrist advocated for the program's foster children at court, in school, and in support of residential placements or special medical care. It was also occasionally necessary to advocate for the agency and its programs within the community.

Many of the roles the child psychiatrist filled for this program could have been filled equally well by a child psychologist or senior social worker with similar competencies, and in fact, services by members of these two professions were incorporated into the team when available. Generally, the program was structured so that the psychiatrist's efforts were complementary to the work of foster parents and caseworkers. Foster parents and caseworkers had access to all available information concerning the foster children, and frequently sat in on psychiatric sessions with the foster child or members of the biological family.

Coordination. The treatment team's coordination of each child's therapy provided the fundamental structure for success within the therapeutic foster care program, which was, by design, open to a wide variety of developmental, family-related, and network influences. Within this flexible milieu, no individual or single professional discipline could provide the amalgam of skills and contacts required by the complex cases typically referred to the program. With care, coordination, and attendant networks of professional and family contacts, the foster parents, caseworkers, and psychiatrist who constituted the core team were able to offer each child a uniquely personal program. Developmental opportunities were provided when and where they were needed in a manner consistent with the child's family background.

Our hope was that over time, as the child matured and his or her family's social networks broadened, both the child and the family might internalize the experiences the program offered. Because years might be required for this process to take place, however, and because society does not stand still to protect any program in the real world, intense coordination and open communication among members of the team were essential in setting up a program for each new case. Until the new, broader patterns of communication became habitual, general principles of confidentiality were always carefully balanced with the demands of present realities. The treatment team could thus support positive individual development and family integrity in a context of cultural and economic realities over long periods of time.

REFERENCES

Bretherton, I., and Walters, E. "Growing Points of Attachment Theory and Research." Monographs of the Society for Research in Child Development, Serial 209, Vol. 20. Chicago: Society for Research in Child Development, 1985.

Burgess, E.W. *Personality and the Social Group.* Chicago: University of Chicago Press, 1929.

Cooley, C.A. *Social Organization.* New York: Scribner's, 1909.

Ekstein, R. *Children of Time and Space, of Action and Impulse.* New York: Appleton-Century-Crofts, 1966.

Fein, E.; Maluccio, A.N.; and Kluger, M. *No More Partings: An Examination of Foster Family Care.* Washington, DC: Child Welfare League of America, 1990.

Fine, P. "Family Networks and Child Psychiatry in a Community Health Project." *Journal of the American Academy of Child Psychiatry* 12, 4 (Oct. 1973): 675-689.

Grossman, K., and Grossman, K. "Attachment Quality as an Organizer of Emotional and Behavioral Responses." In *Attachment Across the Life Cycle,* edited by P. Harris, J. Stevenson-Hinde, and C. Parkes. New York: Routledge Press, 1991, 93-114.

Kohlberg, L. "Revisions in the Theory and Practice of Moral Development." In *New Directions in Child Development: Moral Development,* edited by W. Damon. San Francisco: Jossey-Bass, 1978.

Moncreif, C.M., and Brassard, J.A. "Child Development and Personal Social Networks." *Child Development* 50 (1979): 601-616.

Rae-Grant, N.; Thomas, B.; Offord, D.R.; and Boyle, M.H. "Risk, Protective Factors, and the Prevalence of Behavioral and Emotional Disorders in Children and Adolescents." *Journal of the American Academy of Child and Adolescent Psychiatry* 28, 2 (Nov. 1989): 262-268.

Reiss, D. *The Family's Construction of Reality.* Cambridge, MA: Harvard University Press, 1981.

Scharff, D. "Transference, Countertransference and Technique in Object Relations Family Therapy." In *Foundations of Object Relations Therapy,* edited by J.S. Scharff. Northvale, NJ: Jason Aaronson, 1989.

Schor, E.L. "The Foster Care System and the Health Status of Foster Children." *Pediatrics* 69, 5 (May 1982): 521-528.

Stroufe, L.A. "The Role of Infant-Caregiver Attachment in Development." In *Clinical Implications of Attachment,* edited by J. Belsky and T. Nezworski. Hillsdale, NJ: Erlbaum, 1988.

4. A FOLLOW-UP STUDY OF CASES TREATED

Description of the Study

In 1980 a study was undertaken to appraise eight years of therapeutic foster care under the program outlined in the previous chapters. The study sought to document what type of children and adolescents had been served, to evaluate therapeutic outcomes, and to examine factors associated with success or failure. The data the study set out to obtain are summarized in table 3.

Data were gathered by reviewing the records of 71 children admitted to the program between 1972 and 1980, and supplemented by intensive evaluations of 30 long-term cases. The record review included personal, family, and placement history, mental and physical status over time, and experience in the program. As part of the record review, psychiatric diagnoses were assigned to each case on the five axes of the American Psychiatric Association's Diagnostic and Statistical Manual of Mental Diagnosis-Third Edition (DSM-III), which had recently been developed [APA 1980].

Criteria for inclusion in the 30 intensive evaluations were that the child be at least six years of age, in the program one year or more, and available for clinical follow-up studies. Intensive evaluations consisted of measures of mental status and structured personal interviews that included questions about family history, educational and employment history, social activities, friendships, hobbies, clubs, church attendance, and health, as well as any psychiatric, legal, school, or work difficulties. In addition, all subjects were asked to evaluate their perceived level of attachment to various parent figures, as well as how the program had affected their biological families. Measures of mental status included a condensed

Table 3. Variables Examined in Evaluating Therapeutic Foster Care

Client Characteristics	Foster Parent Characteristics	Program Variables
▪ Sex	▪ Family size	▪ Contact with biological parents
▪ Race	▪ Social class	
▪ Age	▪ Ages	▪ Therapeutic networks
▪ Past history of:	▪ Social networks:	
• Abuse/neglect	• Family	▪ Contact with caseworker
• Incest	• Friends	
• Divorce/Separation	• Neighbors	▪ Contact with mental health workers
• Deaths	▪ Religious affiliation	
▪ Family history	▪ Motivations	▪ Evidence of therapeutic stages
▪ Placement history	▪ Parenting experience	
▪ Behavioral disturbances	▪ Foster care experience	▪ Attendance of foster parents at parent meetings
▪ Psychiatric diagnoses		
▪ Physical-medical illness		

Outcomes
▪ Disposition
▪ Number of program placements
▪ Perception of permanence
▪ Type and number of attachments
▪ Personal attitudes toward foster care
▪ Social adjustment
▪ Developmental disruption and other behavioral ratings
▪ General health

version of the Minnesota Multiphasic Personality Inventory (MMPI-168) and a rating scale that we developed to evaluate symptoms of developmental disruption. Because, on preliminary analysis, the data for this group did not differ significantly from those for the total group of 71 on items from the record review, these cases were thought to adequately represent the group as a whole.

An additional element of the study involved descriptive information about the 28 foster families who had worked most closely with the program. Subjects were selected from a total of 75 families who had participated in the program during the eight years under study on the basis of ability and interest. Data were obtained from semistructured interviews that considered family size, longevity, relationships, socioeconomic factors, parenting and foster parenting experience, motivations, problems, and networks of support.

A computer was used to store data, explore associations between variables, and assist with statistical analysis. Fisher's exact test, the G test, and analysis of covariance were employed as statistical methods [Colton 1974]. Because foster children were admitted for care at different times over the eight-year period, a life table format was selected to express some outcome results in terms of rates rather than average time in placement [Sokal and Rohlf 1969]. Variations in outcome were examined in relationship to characteristics of foster children and foster parents and to factors specific for the program. Tests for statistical significance were set at $p < .05$.

Symptom Evaluation

Clinical experience at the time of the study indicated that a significant proportion of behavioral disturbance in these children was related to disrupted personal development, and that their behaviors were unusually severe, sometimes bizarre, and not well measured by existing instruments. We therefore devised a scale that assessed behavioral symptoms of developmental disruption in order to evaluate the program as treatment (see table 4).

For each of the 30 intensively studied cases, determination of interrater reliability was obtained from correlational analysis of ratings of the symptom clusters outlined in table 4 by two members of the professional team. Each case was rated currently and retrospectively (at intake) as a rough measure of change and

Table 4. The Developmental Disruption Scale

Symptom Cluster

Withdrawal/Inattentiveness: Unreachability, "bad me," rocking, head banging, prolonged whimpering, sleeplessness, fecal hoarding, emotional flatness, prolonged tactile self-stimulation, disinterest in food, gorging on food, pulling and/or eating own hair, general fearfulness, separation terrors, disinterest in play, disinterest in learning and new experiences, disinterest in social companionship.

Attention Demanding/Attacking: Biting, hitting, scratching, kicking, mocking, excessive following, aggressive smearing or discharge of feces or urine, negativism, irritability, poor frustration tolerance, tantrums, impulsivity, distractibility, exhibitionism, noise making, complaining, self-mutilating, sexual assault, firesetting, lying.

Family Disrupting: Complex behavior patterns that cause distrust, shame, and guilt to emerge within the foster family and its network. For example, a foster child might unknowingly share a verbal message with one foster family member while simultaneously generating the opposite acted message with another family member.

Symptom Severity

0	Normal	Abnormal behaviors are essentially absent; child does not present a management problem.
1	Mild	Occasional displays of behavior that are easily managed.
2	Moderate	Significant displays of behavior that are difficult to manage.
3	Severe	Frequent disruptive displays of behavior that are very difficult to manage.
4	Catastrophic	Continuous and overwhelming displays of difficult behaviors.

for cross-tabulation with other variables. Analysis found inter-rater judgments to be highly reliable with respect to each set of current and retrospective scores. Interrater reliability was high-est, however, when scores for three current ratings were averaged and compared for the two raters (R=.94), and when retrospec-tive scores were averaged and compared (R=.88). Current and retrospective measures did not vary significantly among the three subscales. These three subscales were therefore averaged and used as one for subsequent analysis.

Test validity for the Developmental Disruption Scale was evaluated by comparing developmental disruption scores with those obtained for the same cases from the MMPI-168 and the global ratings devised by the psychologist. MMPI data were obtained for 25 children and adolescents who met age and cognitive criteria for testing, and were organized into three standard validity scales and 10 clinical scales by using conversion tables and appropriate adolescent or adult norms [Marks et al. 1974; Newmark et al. 1975; Overall et al. 1976]. The clinical psychologist then assigned a global rating of severity of psychological impairment to each of the 30 cases, using a six-point scale. For the 20 testable cases, global ratings were based upon diagnostic interpretations of the MMPI profile, a review of the case record, results from previ-ous psychological testing, and interviews with foster parents and caseworkers. For the five untestable cases, the procedure was repeated without MMPI results. Subsequent analysis re-vealed significant associations between the psychologist's ratings, MMPI results, and independent ratings of develop-mental disruption in a pattern supporting validity for the Developmental Disruption Scale.

The final step in symptom evaluation involved an inde-pendent set of global ratings taken directly from record reviews and cross-tabulated with other variables from the record review. In this instance, ratings of behavioral improvement and regres-sion were obtained from the records of 63 continuous long-term cases. Ratings from the record review were then compared with independent direct ratings of improvement and regression for the 30 intensively studied children, all of whom were included in the group of 63. In light of the fact that no significant variation was found between the two sets of measures, ratings of improvement or regression from the record reviews were considered adequate for further analysis.

We realize that the measures of behavioral improvement or regression in our study had methodologic limitations. Nevertheless, the research was an honest attempt at objectivity in context, offering at least an estimate of improvement or regression for target symptoms among cases served by the program and enabling us to appraise related factors. In retrospect, we believe that the Developmental Disruption Scale is a reasonable measure of the biobehavioral dysregulation and emotional dissociation obviously present in the population we studied. Such dysfunctions have been more recently described in the literature concerning overwhelming stress [Kolb 1987; Van der Kolk 1987].

The Children Served

Sources of Referral. Eighty-two children and adolescents were referred for treatment under the therapeutic foster care plan—73 by courts, social agencies, community mental health centers, and mental retardation services, and the remainder by relatives and foster or adoptive parents. Most of the children (70%) were referred to the program in a well-planned manner. Some, however, were referred without extensive preliminaries. These referrals usually involved emergencies related to acute child or spouse abuse or parental hospitalization or incarceration. Twenty-one of the children came to the program from group homes and psychiatric hospitals where they had been living for between one month and three years. Eleven of the 82 children evaluated by the program declined placement or returned home within 30 days. These cases were excluded from subsequent analyses; the study focused on the 71 children and adolescents who remained in the program long enough to experience therapeutic care under the criteria described in chapters 2 and 3. These cases are summarized in figure 3 and discussed below.

Sources of referral	A variety of agencies and families
Average age at time of referral	10.2 years
Gender	35 male, 36 female
Ethnicity	44 Caucasian, 22 African American, 5 other
Presenting problems	Conduct problems for 79%, with abuse and neglect in 70% of the cases
Family background	Characterized by instability
Placement history	Most cases had experienced previous placements beginning at age seven
Psychiatric diagnoses	Dominated by conduct and anxiety disorders
Associated chronic medical conditions	Present in 22 cases

Figure 3. Summary Description of 71 Cases Served by the Program

Demographic Characteristics. Age at admission ranged from one year to 17 years, with a mean age of 10.2. Genders were equally represented by 35 males and 36 females. Most of the adolescents were female, while males predominated in the six-to-nine-year-old age group (p<.05). Forty-four of the referred individuals were Caucasian, 22 African American, three Latino, one Native American, and one Asian. African Americans were somewhat overrepresented in the treatment group when compared to the general population of this geographic area, which was less than 10% African American in the 1970 census.

Presenting Problems. Conduct problems were the primary reason for referral for 79% of the treatment group, and most youngsters who had been referred because of misconduct were in state or county custody. A history of abuse and/or neglect was alleged in over 70% of these cases, and 15% were known to have experienced incest. Abuse usually was thought to have occurred in the biological family home, where parents typically exhibited loss of control, inability to set limits, immaturity, or lack of ability to care for the child's special physical or emotional needs.

45

Personal problems on the part of the parents, such as mental or physical illness, were considered the primary reason for referral for the remaining 21% of the cases. Children who had been referred primarily because their parents had problems tended to be younger and less likely to be in state or county custody. They also were more likely to have been admitted during the first two years of the program and to have a history of fewer and less intensive placements.

Family Histories. Family histories were characterized by instability. Fewer than 50% of the records contained any evidence of stable single- or two-parent nuclear family structures. Most of the young people in the treatment program had been separated from one or both parents due to divorce (44%) or death (11%). Twenty-one percent of their mothers had never been wed. In addition, parents were unknown to a subgroup of four children who had been placed in out-of-home care at birth and had experienced between five and 14 placements in various foster homes and institutions before entering the program.

Among cases where the biological parents were known, over 75% had come from low-income socioeconomic backgrounds. Family sizes averaged five members for the same 75%. Parental histories typically included the death or divorce of parents, family alcoholism, psychiatric involvement, and childhood foster care placement. Parents reported personal physical or sexual abuse as children in 7% of the cases. Ten percent of the parents were diagnosed as having a major psychiatric disorder, and 7% were undergoing treatment for substance abuse and/or dependence.

Placement Histories Prior to Admission. Previous placements were the norm for children and adolescents treated in our program. A total of 165 previous placements and re-placements were reported in the case records of 55 of the 71 children studied. Of this group of 55, 44% had been placed three times or more. The ages at which these youngsters had first been removed from the biological or adoptive home ranged from birth to 16 years, with an average age of 7.4 years (sd + 4.8) at time of first placement for the total group, and 7.0 years (sd + 4.6) for children with a history of multiple placements.

Combinations of long- and short-term placements in both foster homes and institutions were not uncommon among the children studied. Seventy-eight percent had a history of placements in juvenile centers, psychiatric hospitals, and group homes. Placements of under three months in psychiatric hospitals had occurred principally among individuals who had behavioral or developmental disorders. Histories of long-term psychiatric hospitalization were more frequent among foster children with mental retardation, developmental disabilities, or other disabling physical disorders. Three children presented records of repeated short-term nonpsychiatric hospitalization, and three had experienced long-term hospitalization for chronic illnesses.

Psychiatric Diagnoses.* All except two of the 71 foster children had one or more Axis I psychiatric disorders, according to DSM-III criteria, and one-third had two or more psychiatric disorders. Conduct disorder was the most frequent diagnosis, involving 46% of the population. Anxiety disorder, also a frequent diagnosis, was found in 20% of the population, particularly among children who were under five years of age at the time of admission. Other psychiatric diagnoses were adjustment disorder, attention deficit disorder, oppositional disorder, major depressive disorder, and pervasive developmental disorder. Three cases of organic personality disorder were diagnosed, in association with evidence of diffuse brain damage, epilepsy, and a congenital brain anomaly, respectively. Eighteen percent of the cases had some degree of mental retardation (four cases mild, seven moderate, one severe, and two borderline). Enuresis and/or encopresis were present in 14% of the population.

---

* Most of the diagnoses in the study involved conversion of outmoded DSM-II categories from the record review into the then-current DSM-III categories. In light of present knowledge, were the evaluations done today, we probably would have diagnosed more specifically for cases of post-traumatic stress, substance abuse, panic, dissociative disorder, attachment disorder, and teratogenic disorders.

Specific developmental disorders were diagnosed in 25 of the 71 children. Foster children with developmental disorders received concurrent diagnoses of mental retardation, attention deficit disorder, or neurological disorder more frequently than did the other children. Children with developmental disorders were significantly more likely to be male, to have been in state or county custody at the time of admission, and to have a major chronic physical disorder. They were also likely to have been removed from the biological home at a younger age than the group as a whole (5.6 years vs. 7.4 years) and to have had significantly more and longer placements than other children.

Associated Medical Conditions. Thirty-one percent of the children also carried a diagnosis of one or more serious nonpsychiatric medical disorders. Associated nonpsychiatric diagnoses included leukemia, paraplegia, diffuse encephalopathy, congenital brain damage, congenital heart disease, cranial anomaly, hydrocephalus, scoliosis, spina bifida, cerebral palsy, cystic fibrosis, asthma, Ehlers-Danlos Syndrome, diabetes mellitus, and hypothyroidism. Two children required surgery for pathological eye conditions, and one child was status post-ileostomy. Epilepsy was documented in 10% of the cases. Recurrent infections of the middle ear, respiratory tract, urinary tract, and kidneys were frequent among the population, and other comparatively minor medical problems were present in 13% of the cases. Moreover, 53% of the children were receiving prescription medications, which included psychostimulants for 17%, neuroleptics (major tranquilizers) for 13%, anticonvulsants for 13%, anxiolytics (minor tranquilizers) for 9%, antidepressants for 6%, and insulin for 3%.

Measures of Stress and Adaptation

DSM-III Ratings. Ratings of psychosocial stress and adaptive functioning were made according to Axis IV and Axis V in DSM-III. As figure 4 illustrates, over half of the 71 cases had experienced severe to catastrophic conditions of stress in the year prior to diagnosis, and adaptive functioning was typically poor.

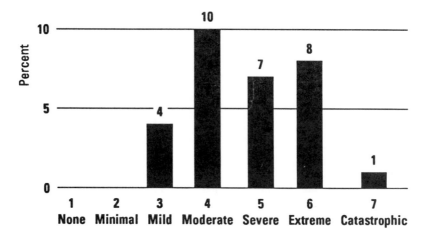

Figure 4(a). Severity of Psychosocial Stressors (DSM-III, Axis IV) in the Year Prior to Admission for 30 Follow-Up Cases

Developmental Disruption. The average combined intake score for symptoms of developmental disruption for the intensively studied subgroup of 30 was 2.23+.15. This score is about midway on the scale shown in table 4, and indicates moderate to severe symptoms of developmental disruption.

Results of Psychological Evaluations for 30 Follow-up Cases. Fourteen of the 24 children from the intensively studied group of 30 who were testable with the MMPI-168 had scales in the range of clinical pathology, eight others showed subclinical elevations, and only two lacked scale elevations. Scale profiles presented no typical pattern, except for eight cases who had clinically elevated F scales, essentially a measure of emotional turmoil. This group consisted of white adolescents who had been removed from their biological families early in life and had experienced many subsequent placements. The other six of the 14 tended to be younger and to have histories of abuse. The ten cases with subclinical ele-

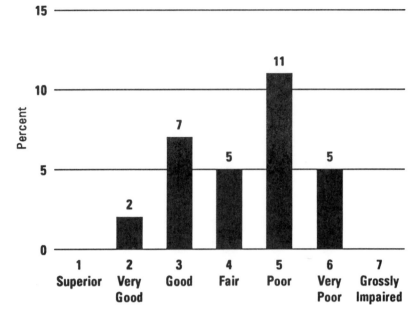

Figure 4(b). Highest Level of Adaptive Functioning (DSM-III, Axis V) in the Year Prior to Admission for 30 Follow-Up Cases

vations included six out of the nine children and adolescents with chronic physical illnesses. Children in this group had been placed less frequently than the group as a whole.

The psychologist's global ratings of overall severity of psychological impairment for the follow-up group of 30 individuals described 6% as very severe, 33.3% as severe, 20% as moderately severe, 26.7% as mild, and 13.3% as showing traits of disturbance only. None rated free of disturbance.

Despite the relatively small sample, the statistical relationship between global ratings of psychopathology and certain placement factors was remarkable. The highest correlation was between the global rating of psychopathology and the total number of placements experienced in foster care and institutions ($r=.44$, $p<.05$). This association persisted when the influence of age and length of time in placement was controlled through first-order partial correlations for age ($r=.38$, $p<.05$)

and for length of time in placement (r=.36, p<.05). Psychopathology also correlated with an older age at admission to therapeutic foster care (r=.37, p<.05) and with more years in placement prior to admission (r=.31, p<.05). Correlations of psychopathology at borderline significance included age at first removal from the home (r=.10), number of placements in our therapeutic foster care program (r=.01), and length of time within the therapeutic program (r=.24).

REFERENCES

American Psychiatric Association. *Diagnostic and Statistical Manual of Mental Disorders,* 3rd ed. Washington, DC: American Psychiatric Association, 1980.

Colton, T. *Statistics in Medicine.* Boston: Little, Brown and Co., 1974.

Kolb, L.C. "A Neuropsychological Hypothesis Explaining Post-Traumatic Stress Disorders." *American Journal of Psychiatry* 144, 8 (Aug. 1987): 989-995.

Marks, P.A.; Seeman, W.; and Haller, D.L. *The Actuarial Use of the MMPI with Adolescents and Adults.* Baltimore: Williams and Wilkins, 1974.

Newmark, C.S.; Newmark, L.; and Cook, L. "The MMPI-168 with Psychiatric Patients." *Journal of Clinical Psychology* 31, 1 (Jan. 1975): 61-64.

Overall, J.E.; Higgins, W.; and DeSchweinitz, A. "Comparison of Differential Diagnostic Discrimination for Abbreviated and Standard MMPI." *Journal of Clinical Psychology* 32, 2 (Apr. 1976): 237-245.

Sokal, R.R., and Rohlf, F.J. *Biometry.* San Francisco: W.H. Freeman & Co., 1969.

Van der Kolk, B.A. *Psychological Trauma.* Washington, DC: American Psychiatric Press, 1987.

5. THERAPEUTIC OUTCOMES

Certain variables from the record review of 71 cases were examined for indicators of a therapeutic process and positive or negative outcomes related to treatment: continuity within the program, case plans for long-term permanency, behavioral improvement or regression, and stages of therapy during placement. Additional variables examined in the more intensive study of 30 cases included personal adjustment, parental attachment, disposition, and changes in symptoms of developmental disruption. A brief follow-up for network and disposition factors was also conducted in 1982.

Results from the Record Review

Placement Continuity. A fundamental goal of our program was to help disturbed foster children and adolescents establish stable, ongoing therapeutic relationships with foster parents. In light of the fact that our population typically had placement difficulties prior to referral and was characterized by lifelong problems, the program was reasonably successful at ensuring placement continuity. In a total of 90 placements in 53 foster homes involving 71 children and adolescents, only one child experienced more than two therapeutic placements. Seventy-one of the placements were initial and 18 were second placements. Ten placements lasted four years or longer.

More often than not, initial placement was only the beginning of a complex case history within the program. Thus, 22 of 71 initial placements were ongoing at the time of the record review in 1980, while 49 were not. Outcomes for these discontinuous placements included three individuals who were adopted by foster parents from the program, ten who returned to their biological families, five who went on to independent living, 15 who entered group homes, psychiatric hospitals, or juvenile centers, one who died of leukemia, and 15 who were placed a second time within the program. In addition to the 15 who experienced second placements directly from their first foster homes, two returned to the program from brief placements in group homes, and one from a psychiatric hospital, which brought the total number of second placements to 18. Of these 18 placements, three were ongoing at the time of the study. In addition, eight of the foster children returned to their biological families from second placements, one was adopted by the foster parents, two went on to independent living, two transferred to group homes, one was hospitalized in a psychiatric facility, and one was placed within the program for a third time. The single third placement was ongoing at the time of the study.

Case Plans. A long-range case plan for family permanency is always desirable, and facilitates emotional stability during therapy. In our study, three plans were identified from case records: (1) a return to the biological family, (2) ongoing foster care leading to legal or de facto adoption, and (3) a flexible approach toward options over time. The life table method of statistical analysis referred to in chapter 4 was used to calculate probabilities for disposition of the 71 cases within a statistically projected limit of four years. Results suggested that the program conformed reasonably well to its initial case plans for ultimate disposition.

The initial plan in 30 cases was for the foster child to return to the biological family under improved conditions. Children in this group typically suffered from conduct disorders, stressful home environments, and parents with poor coping skills. All 30 were in the legal custody of their biological parents at the time of initial placement within the program, and had comparatively limited histories of previous placements. Although this group had a high probability (59%) of returning to their biological families and a low probability (8%) of remaining in foster care, they also had a 44% probability of a second placement within the program, and a 25% probability of transfer to a psychiatric hospital or group home.

The initial plan for 12 cases was stable, ongoing family foster care or adoption. All of the children in this group were in state custody at the time of placement; most had lost contact with their biological families and four had never known their parents. Their complex histories included placement and re-placement in a variety of foster and group homes, psychiatric hospitals, and other institutions, and a high prevalence of learning disabilities, neurological disorders, mental retardation, and special physical needs was evident. These children were highly likely (72%) to experience ongoing care within the program for the projected period of four years, with virtually no probability of returning to a biological family, and little likelihood (12%) of a second placement with the program. They did, however, have a 28% probability of transferring to a group home.

The initial case plan for the remaining 29 cases was flexible and open-ended. This group was notable for clear-cut histories of abuse and neglect, behavior problems, previous placements, and active court involvement. Individuals with flexible case plans carried a 21% probability of returning to the biological family, a 28% probability of long-term foster or adoptive care, a 25% probability of placement in a second home under the program, and a 21% probability of transfer to a group home or hospital within four years.

Behavioral Improvement. Behavioral improvement following placement within the program was considered as evidence that therapy had been effective. Therefore, as outlined in chapter 4, case notes were reviewed and data compiled concerning behavioral improvement, stability, or deterioration between the time of entry into the program and the time of the study in 1980. Upon analysis of the 62 cases of children who had been in the program at least one year, which was considered the minimum length of time necessary to have experienced therapy as described in chapter 2, 74% were found to have improved behaviorally, 25% were unchanged, and none were worse.

Marked improvement, which was found in 48% of the cases, was significantly more frequent when the foster children were relatively young, had come from relatively stable, low-income socioeconomic backgrounds, and had been placed in the program voluntarily while in the legal custody of the parents. There were

Table 5. Serious Behavioral Incidents in 90

Longevity of placements	Number of placements ongoing at the beginning of each period	Number of incidents per time period
0-3 months	90	19
3-6 months	78	14
6-9 months	73	11
9-12 months	57	7
13-15 months	48	16
15-18 months	36	4
18-21 months	30	1
21-14 months	29	4
25-27 months	21	3
27-30 months	20	1
30-33 months	18	0
33-36 months	15	1
37-39 months	14	2
39-42 months	12	0
42-45 months	10	1
45-48 months	10	2

also statistical trends for diagnoses of developmental and neurological disorders among these children. Statistical trends for little behavioral improvement were evident when the young people were adolescent, had come from middle-class backgrounds and unstable homes, and had a diagnosis of conduct disorder.

Stages of Placement. The record review also sought to verify the clinical impression that predictable stages occur during therapeutic placement and that such stages are punctuated by emotional crises with behavioral acting out. Anticipated stages included an initial honeymoon followed by a crisis of acceptance after two or three months, followed by another period of stability, which, after several more months, would lead to a crisis of belonging followed by relative stability [Fine 1985].

To explore this clinical hypothesis, data were compiled during the record review to document behavioral incidents seri-

Therapeutic Placements for 71 Children

Percent of incidents per placement per time period	Number of placements with incidents that led to placement disruption per time period	Percent of placement disruptions per time period
21.6	5	5.5
18.1	3	3.8
16.1	5	6.8
14.4	1	1.8
34.8	4	8.3
11.3	2	5.5
3.3	0	0
15.1	2	6.8
14.3	1	4.8
5.3	0	0
0	0	0
6.7	0	0
14.8	1	7.1
0	0	0
10.0	0	0
20.0	1	10.0

ous enough to threaten the foster child's relationship with the foster parents or placement within the foster home. Pooled data for 90 therapeutic placements involving 71 foster children were then organized into sequential three-month segments, regardless of the month or year when the behavioral incident had occurred. Actual placement disruptions were also compiled in the same manner. Results are shown in table 5.

As this table shows, a clear pattern of serious behavioral incidents became apparent when the number of incidents was analyzed in proportion to the number of placements during each time increment, and there was a rough parallel between behavioral incidents and placement disruptions. As figure 5 illustrates, however, the actual pattern differed from our clinical hypothesis. There was no honeymoon, and the percentage of serious incidents per placement increased approximately yearly, initially between 13 and

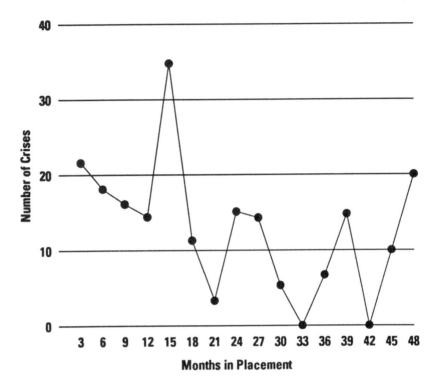

Figure 5. Serious Behavioral Incidents in Proportion to the Total Number of Placements during Each Time Increment of Placement for 90 Therapeutic Placements Involving 71 Children

15 months, and, to a lesser degree, between 21 and 27 months, between 36 and 39 months, and again at 48 months.

These data were interpreted as consistent with the presence of an increased intensity of relationships between foster children and therapeutic foster parents at the end of the first year and each year thereafter.

Results from Follow-Up Interviews

Results from follow-up interviews with the 30 children in the sample were consistent with improvements noted in the record review. The average age of the foster children interviewed was 14.6 years. Interviews included 16 children with ongoing placements in the program and four who had been adopted by therapeutic foster parents. For these 20 children, an average of four years had elapsed since initial admission into the program. The other 10 children had left the program an average of 2.7 years before the interview. Five had returned to the biological family, one was living independently, two were in community group homes, one was in a correctional institution, and the other was in a state-run residential center. Results from each section of the interview are reported below.

Health and Personal Problems. The group as a whole continued to have problems with health and personal adjustment at the time of the follow-up interview. Twenty-three of the young people reported that they were in good physical health, and the remaining seven admitted to benign intermittent physical illness. Their subjective impression of physical well-being notwithstanding, nine of the respondents had been hospitalized during the previous six months, three as a result of injury or accident, five due to a chronic physical illness, and one for a psychiatric evaluation. Moreover, six individuals had received prescription medications; one because of psychiatric indications and five for other medical reasons.

Nine of the group reported adjustment problems during the previous year, four of which were considered serious. Two individuals had received failing grades at school, four had lost jobs, and three had been arrested for minor law violations. One other individual had been expelled from school following repeated suspensions, and had been arrested for burglarizing his adoptive home. All of these problems were found among the 14 individuals who had left the program. No problems with school, employment, or legal authorities were reported by the 16 individuals who were still in therapeutic care under the program.

Social Relationships. Most members of the follow-up group reported a remarkably positive level of social adjustment considering the serious nature of their initial problems. Twenty-six were attending public schools at the time of the interview, 18 in regular classrooms and eight in special education. Three others had completed high school, and one was attending a community college. Ten also held full- or part-time jobs.

Twenty individuals reported that they attended church frequently, often with their foster parents, and 15 described hobbies that involved peers or activities outside the foster home, including roller skating, swimming, chess, camping, and team sports. Eleven youths belonged to clubs and recreational programs such as the YMCA, Sertoma Club, and Boys Club. Fourteen others listed only home-centered activities, such as watching television, reading, listening to music, or playing with dolls, and one said that she engaged in no social activities.

In terms of peer relationships, 27 said they had a "best friend" in their age group, and 13 a "close friend" of the opposite sex. Only three individuals, two of whom had neurological handicaps, said they had no close friends. These three also reported that they had poor relationships with their foster parents as well as their biological parents.

Relationships with Foster and Biological Families. Positive relationships with both the foster and biological families were considered desirable. On the basis of these follow-up interviews, the program was relatively successful in this regard. Twenty-five respondents said that they had been able to establish a supportive relationship with a foster family. Only three reported a poor relationship, and two an indifferent relationship.

Interviewers also asked each young person about his or her current relationship with the biological family and how the program had affected it. Among the 26 individuals who remembered their biological families, a majority of the follow-up group said that they had a good relationship with family members, and that therapeutic foster care had helped the relationship prosper. Table 6 details these perceptions.

As the table shows, 16 of 26 individuals considered the current relationship with their biological family to be a good one. Ten of the 16 said that foster care had improved this relationship, and five claimed that it had no effect. In addition, one boy, a Native American who was living with his biological fami-

Table 6. Perceptions of 26 Adolescents Regarding Their Relationship with Their Biological Family and the Effect of Therapeutic Foster Care on This Relationship

	Good	Indifferent or ambiguous	Poor	Total	Percent
Improved	10	3	1	14	53.9
No Effect	5	3	2	10	38.4
Harmed	1	1	0	2	7.7
Total	16	7	3	26	100.0
Percent	61.5	26.9	11.6	100	

ly at the time of the interview, said that he had been able to maintain a good relationship with his own family, but that his experience in family foster care had made the relationship more difficult. He said that he had not been able to see his family often enough, and that foster family members had referred to his grandmother as "an alcoholic."

Seven of the young people claimed to be indifferent about their biological families. One said that, although she felt indifferent, therapeutic care had actually helped, because it had taught her that "a kid isn't a parent." Another said that placement had given her a chance "to get away for awhile," and a third said that foster care had improved her ability to communicate. Three others, all siblings, said that the program had not affected the family relationship one way or another, and one felt that the experience had interfered with his connection to biological relatives. He was a mentally retarded, physically abused boy who had lost all contact with his biological family; although he had been adopted by his foster parents, he had burglarized their home and was removed.

The remaining four foster children said that their current relationship with their biological family was poor. Two indicated that foster care had not affected their feelings about their relatives one way or the other, one said that a constructive experience in foster care had helped him decide not to return to his biological family, and the third said that a positive relationship with his previous foster family had helped him cope with living at his biological parent's home.

Emotional Attachments to Parents. Two additional items from the follow-up interviews provided data suggesting that close emotional attachments developed between foster children and foster parents in the program, and that these attachments were typically not at the expense of relationships with biological parents. Each of the 30 foster children was asked which parental figure he or she felt most closely attached to, and with whom the terms *mother* and *father* were most closely associated. Thirteen responded that they felt most closely attached to the foster parents, nine to the biological parents, and three to both sets of parents. Five individuals, four of whom were older adolescents, refused to say that they were closely attached to either set of parents; two indicated attachment to a grandparent, and one to a caseworker. In terms of whom they considered "mother" and "father," 11 most closely associated those words with foster parents, four with biological parents, and 13 with both. Two other individuals refused to associate the terms *mother* and *father* with either set of parents. One facetiously identified two caseworkers as her mother and father, and the other simply said "No one."

There were also indications that graduation from the therapeutic program resulted in continuous supportive relationships with previous foster parents. Nine of ten individuals who had left therapeutic homes at the time of the interview indicated that the foster parents continued to be psychologically important, and the five individuals who were living with biological parents at the time of the interview identified both the biological parents and the foster parents as psychologically important.

Outcomes: Reducing Symptoms of Developmental Disruption

Reducing symptoms of developmental disruption by means of corrective parenting was a basic goal of the program. We measured changes in symptoms by comparing average scores on the five-point Developmental Disruption Scale described in chapter 4 both at intake and during the follow-up evaluation in 1980. According to the ratings, the group of 30 follow-up cases improved by almost one full point on the five-point scale. The average score at intake was 2.26±.15, indicating moderate symptoms, while the average score at follow-up was 1.35±.14, indicative of mild symptoms. The average amount of improvement was .91±.13.

Extensive cross-tabulations were run to compare average improvement for the group as a whole with improvement based on average scores for items on the record review and the follow-up study. Despite limitations inherent in this approach, the findings represent an encouraging affirmation that stable therapeutic foster placements can result in symptom reduction.

Scores on four items were found to differ with statistical significance from those of the group as a whole; two indicated more improvement, and two less improvement. As illustrated in table 7, significant improvement was present among youths who said that they felt most attached to therapeutic foster parents, as well as those who were in ongoing placements with therapeutic foster parents or who had been adopted by them. In contrast, significantly less improvement was found among youths who had returned to their family of origin or had a preadmission history of long-term psychiatric hospitalization or group home placement.

Other correlations between improvement on developmental disruption scores and items from the record review were not statistically significant. However, some trends toward significance were present and may shed light on indications for this particular type of program. Specifically, there were trends toward above-average improvement for individuals with established histories of abuse and neglect who were Caucasian, were less than 14 years old, and had experienced long-term foster care prior to admission into the program. In contrast, statistical trends toward lower average improvement scores were present among youths who were non-Caucasian, were

Table 7. Improvement in Average Scores for Develop-
and Average Scores for Improvement by Subgroups

Variable
Total Sample

■ Youths most attached to foster parents
■ Youths in ongoing placement or adopted by foster parents
■ Youths who had returned to their biological families
■ Youths with a preadmission history of long-term psychiatric or group home placements

■ Caucasians
  • Less than age 14
  • Established history of abuse and neglect
  • A history of long-term foster care prior to admission
■ Other Ethnic Groups
  • 14 to 17 years of age
  • Initial case plan of return to biological family

■ Organic personality disorder
■ Attention deficit disorder
■ Neurologic disorder
■ Developmental disorder
■ Adjustment disorder
■ Conduct disorder

mid-adolescent, and had an initial case plan of return to the biological family.

Statistical trends toward significant differences from the total group were also present when improvement on scores for developmental disruption was cross-tabulated by diagnostic categories. The bottom of table 7 shows that diagnostic categories with statistical trends toward higher-than-average improvement included organic personality disorder, neurological disorder, developmental

mental Disruption from Intake for 30 Cases in 1980,
That Differed Significantly from the Total Group

Number of Cases	Average Preadmission Rating	Average Improvement
30	2.26 ± .15	.91 ± .13*
17	2.28 ± .21	1.21 ± .15
22	2.19 ± .19	1.03 ± .14
5	2.23 ± .23	.33 ± .38
45	2.37 ± .19	.70 ± .22
18	2.58 ± .16*	1.16 ± .14
10	2.33 ± .21	1.06 ± .14
17	2.38 ± .21	1.07 ± .25
12	2.19 ± .30	1.03 ± .17
12	1.78 ± .22	.54 ± .20
14	2.01 ± .24	.75 ± .16
9	2.48 ± .17	.78 ± .27
2	3.25 ± .25	2.00 ± .17
3	2.89 ± .20	1.28 ± .05
7	2.86 ± .20*	1.17 ± .29
16	2.79 ± .12*	1.07 ± .18
4	1.54 ± .39	.42 ± .24
12	2.08 ± .19	.79 ± .2

*p<.05

disorder, and attention-deficit disorder. In contrast, diagnostic categories with a statistical trend toward less improvement included adjustment disorder and conduct disorder. Thus, indications are that our psychiatrically oriented therapeutic foster care program was particularly effective for children and young adolescents with brain-related and developmental disorders, and less successful for those with habitual conduct disorders and intermittent exposure to stressful family situations.

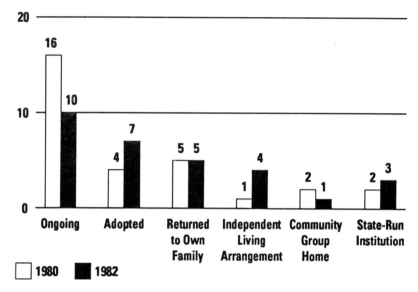

Figure 6. Dispositional Outcome for 30 Cases Followed Up in 1980 and 1982

Further Disposition and Continuity

Disposition. The final element of our study was a brief follow-up of the same group of 30 two years later when their average age was close to 17. The purpose of this follow-up was to evaluate further changes in disposition and continuity of relationships. Figure 6 illustrates that ten individuals remained in therapeutic foster homes in 1982, six fewer than in 1980. Meanwhile, three more had been adopted, for a total of seven, and three had gone on to independent living, for a total of four youths who were living on their own at the time of the second follow-up study. The number who had returned to the biological family remained constant at five.

Not surprisingly, the lifelong perturbations that characterized the group as a whole continued during the two years that the program was winding down. For example, the five children living with biological parents in 1982 were not the same five who had been with their biological families in 1980; by 1982, three of the original five were at state-run psychiatric or juvenile facilities and two were living independently.

Table 8. Contact with Foster and Biological Families for 30 Follow-Up Cases in 1982

Disposition 1982	Number of cases	Regular contact with biological family	Regular contact with foster family	No memory of biological family
▪ Ongoing in placement	10	10	9	0
▪ Adopted by foster parents	7	0	7	3
▪ Living with biological family	5	5	5	0
▪ Living at institution or independently	8	6	5	1
Total	30	21	26	4

Continuing Relationships. Follow-up interviews in 1982 revealed a continued investment in therapeutic foster parents by youngsters after they had left the foster home, as well as the continuation of relationships with biological family members. As shown in table 8, 11 of the 13 youngsters who were no longer living with foster parents (those living with biological families and those living at an institution or independently) said that they nevertheless maintained contact with them. By the same token, nine out of ten youths who remained in therapeutic foster homes and had not been adopted maintained regular contact with their biological parents. However, none of the seven youths who had been adopted by foster parents was in close contact with the biological family. This group included three of the four individuals who had no memory of a biological family and three African American siblings who had resisted adoption and avowed continued loyalty to their lost biological family.

REFERENCE

Fine, P. "Clinical Aspects of Foster Care." In *Foster Care: Current Issues, Policies , and Practices*, edited by M.J. Cox and R.D. Cox. Norwood, NJ: Ablex Publishing Corp., 1985.

6. FOSTER PARENTS AS THERAPISTS

Foster parents in our program typically demonstrated certain abilities that went beyond their collaboration with the therapeutic team or their role as heads of households. This chapter describes and analyzes various characteristics of exemplary foster families in the program, the techniques they used, and the qualities they possessed that may be related to successful therapeutic foster care.

Characteristics of Selected Foster Families

Twenty-eight of the 75 foster families who worked with the program during its first 10 years of operation were included in this facet of our study. Families chosen had been connected with the program for at least one year and were available for interviews in 1981. Interviews were conducted with the foster mother from each family by one or two staff members, using a 40-category questionnaire. The average foster mother who participated in the interviews had completed 11.9 years of school, and her average age when interviewed was 45.6 years. Results are summarized in figure 7.

The average foster family in the study group consisted of six members (5.7 + 2.3), not including foster children. Seventy-five percent were headed by married couples, 10% by widows, and the remainder by other single women (15%). Among foster parents who were married, the average duration of marriage was 21 years (20.8 + 9.5, range 1 to 37 yrs.). Boys and girls were represented in about equal proportions among children in the families.

The group was mainly middle class; 89% of the wage earners were in blue-collar or clerical positions, and 11% were in administrative positions. Their average income in 1981 was $19,990, not including foster care payments, and 64% of the families earned between $15,000 and $30,000. Three families reported incomes of under $10,000, one was on welfare, and one

---

- Headed by a couple who have been married 21 years
- Six family members, with boys and girls in equal proportions
- Urban location
- Nonminority status
- Blue-collar or clerical employment
- Low-average income
- Network of 90 extended family members
- Active church membership
- Eventful life experiences
- Parents spend moderate amounts of time away from children

Figure 7. Characteristics of the Average Therapeutic Foster Family (Sample of 28)

reported an income of over $45,000. Sixty-one percent of the foster families identified themselves as Caucasian, 30% as African American, and 7% as Latino. The remaining 3% were of other ethnicities. Seventy-five percent lived in a medium-sized urban area, 21% in a suburb, and 3% in a rural area. Thirty-six percent of the parents said that they knew all of their neighbors well, 39% reported that they knew selected neighbors well, and 25% said that they were familiar with only a few.

A review of the literature indicated that the foster parents in our therapeutic program were generally similar in terms of family size, education, marital status, ethnicity, and employment to foster parents described in other studies [Bauer and Heinke 1976; Carbino 1980; Hampson and Tavormina 1981; Paulson et al. 1974; Petersen and Pierce 1974]. Additional insights about our particular group of foster parents emerged from their answers to a survey concerning supportive relationships, motivation, experience, treatment effectiveness, and therapeutic technique.

Supportive Relationships. The results of our survey indicated that extended family relationships were important to the foster parents in our program. The average parent in the group listed 89 relatives as members of the extended family network, and the size of these networks ranged from 14 to 250 members. Eighty-nine percent of the foster parents reported that they routinely spent time with relatives. For 56%, contact with extended family members was frequent, and for 79%, it was face-to-face rather than restricted to telephone conversations. Only 11% of the foster parents said that they rarely or never spent time with relatives.

Church attendance was also important for members of this group. Seventy-one percent were Protestant, 21% Catholic, and 7% had no church affiliation. Thirty-nine percent of the 28 respondents were active members of charismatic churches. Attendance at church was frequent for 61% of the foster parents, occasional for 29%, and infrequent for 11%.

Personal time played an important, but not overriding, role for the foster mothers. All said that they spent personal time away from children, and for 39%, this was "a lot of the time." None reported that they spent most of their time alone, and none said that they seldom spent time alone. For 89% of the group, personal time was frequently spent with their husband or another close family member, and for 71% it was shared with a friend. The average number of close friends was five, and the range of close friends was between one and eight.

As another aspect of the research, each foster parent completed a survey of 43 important life events [Holmes et al. 1967]. The survey was divided into two sections—first, all items were responded to in terms of the preceding 12 months, and then in terms of lifetime events before the preceding year. Results indicated that foster parents in this program had eventful, often stressful lives, but remained committed to their families even during periods of continual stress. According to a scale that accompanied the survey, 11% had accumulated enough stressors during the previous 12 months to predict an 80% probability of stress-related physical illness, and 36% had accumulated enough stressors to predict a 50% chance of illness. With regard to specific stressful life events during the previous 12 months, 36% reported the death of a close friend or relative, 25% a serious illness or injury within the family, 14% a significant financial reversal, and 7% notable litigation. Only one foster parent had

- Affirmative ideology
- Child-centered motivations
- Licensed by more than one agency
- Eight years of foster care experience with 28 children and adolescents
- Four foster children currently in the home
- No age or gender preference in foster children
- Professionalism: detailed attention to each foster child's progress
- Therapeutic fostering perceived as reinforcing existing family values

Figure 8. Experience and Motivation of the Average Therapeutic Foster Care Families (Sample of 28)

been divorced during the year, and another had been separated from her husband.

Results from the scale for lifetime events were similar to those for the previous year. Stressful events had been frequent, and fully 86% of the foster parents reported that they had experienced the death of a close relative or friend during their lifetime. Only 17% reported a divorce prior to the current marriage.

Motivation. Data indicating constructive motivation, relevant experience, and professionalism among foster parents in our program are listed in figure 8.

Each foster parent in the study was surveyed on a 17-item list of motivations for fostering. The average member of the group specified three reasons for fostering, and there was a range of between one and five responses. Fully 96% specified an ideological reason, such as charity, ethics, or religious values, and for 68%, the ideological motivation was primary. The second most popular motivation for fostering, found in 50% of the group, was a desire to raise children, and 21% said that this reason was primary. Typical answers in this category included, "I know how to raise children," "We love children," "We have enough love to go around," "Our children were grown, and we wanted more," and "We wanted a playmate for our child." Other less prevalent reasons for fostering included an inability to conceive biological children (18%), attraction to a particular child (7%), a desire to replace a child who had died (7%), knowing friends or relatives who had been foster children (11%), and having been raised as a foster child (4%). Only two of the foster parents cited pecuniary considerations as a major reason for fostering, and one felt that she had been pressured to participate in the program by a caseworker.

Experience. Our study group was unusually experienced at foster parenting. On average, they had been raising foster children for eight years (7.6 yrs. + 5.3), with a range of between 1 and 30 years. A typical member of the group had been licensed for six years (5.7 yrs + 3.5), although many of the parents had taken a foster child into their homes before they were formally licensed. The average number of children fostered over time was 28 (27.8 + 40.9), with a range between one and 155. As a group, they had fostered a grand total of 733 children.

Foster parents in our program typically took their work as therapists seriously. Most (74%) said that they kept ongoing personal records about the progress of each child, usually in the form of a scrapbook. Fully 96% reported that they attended some or all of the monthly support group meetings. The average number of meetings attended during the 12 months prior to the study had been eight (7.7 + 4.2), with a range of between 0 and 12.

The group as a whole expressed an interest in treating children of all ages and both sexes. Four said that they preferred boys, three preferred girls, and 19 had no gender preference. Only one foster parent said she preferred babies; ten (37%) preferred younger children, five preferred preteens, three preferred teenagers, and eight expressed no preference by age group. The average number of foster children in the foster parents' homes at the time of the survey was four (3.5 + 2.4), with a range between one and ten.

Effects of Fostering on the Foster Family. Responses received when foster parents were asked to describe the effect therapeutic parenting had on their families reinforced the impression of constructive motivations in the face of an intrinsically stressful endeavor. Eighty-six percent reported that the effect on their family had been essentially positive, 7% indicated

73

that it had been negative, and 7% said that it had been neutral. However, 33% of those who described a generally positive experience also specified negative aspects.

The most frequent positive perception of the effect of fostering on the foster family, mentioned by 63%, was that it was a growth experience for the families' own children. Other frequent positive perceptions were that fostering provided a growth experience for the foster parents themselves (43%), or for the family as a whole (36%). Representative positive comments included, "It brought us a lot of happiness, giving and getting love," "It helped our children be more empathic and respectful to the family," "I became more aware of cruelties in the world today, and our family now appreciates their closeness," "It helped me increase communication with my husband and for the kids to learn patience," and "It helped my children be more responsible."

Negative perceptions about the experience also focused on the effects it had on the foster families' children (40%), the family as a unit (40%), and on the foster parents themselves (20%). Typical negative comments included, "It was hard on our youngest," "It alienated the oldest," "We had to give up some activities because of the foster children's behavior," "It changed our lifestyle to be less spontaneous," and "I was personally exasperated when I couldn't seem to help them change."

It was partly because of the foster parents' concerns about their biological children that two series of group meetings were held weekly for a period of three months each during 1980 and 1981. Sixteen biological children between the ages of nine and 17 years participated in the meetings; their parents did not attend. First, the youngsters discussed their feelings about foster care with members of the therapeutic team, and then they elected to produce two autodocumentary tapes with similar themes. Essentially, the tapes convey the impression that having foster children in their homes was embarrassing, difficult, and disruptive. Yet positive values won out in the end, and an enduring bond of loyalty formed between foster and biological children in these homes. Staff members from the program and foster parents were generally impressed with how accurate these children were in their depictions of the roles and attitudes of parents, social workers, school personnel, foster children, and members of the foster children's biological families. Moreover, their portrayal of psychiatric syndromes and specific effects of learning disabilities on dialogue was often uncanny in its accuracy The children who produced these dramatizations unequivocally perceived their parents as therapists for the foster children. They also perceived themselves as playing a therapeutic role, usually as mentors or critics. The children who participated in these meetings typically reported that the weekly group sessions helped their morale by providing camaraderie with other young people from similar situations as well as an opportunity for self-expression. Their parents generally agreed.

Indicators for Placement Stability and Treatment Effectiveness

One final goal of our interviews with foster parents was to seek cross-correlations with an indicator of placement stability and behavioral improvement. The proportion of disrupted placements for 21 of the foster families who had worked with 29 foster children from the program for at least one year before 1980 was cross-tabulated with the proportion of disrupted placements for children in families from the same group as a function of each item on the follow-up survey. The average improvement on scores for developmental disruption for the 29 foster children in the 21 families was then cross-tabulated with the average amount of improvement for children who scored positively on each item from the follow-up survey. Table 9 shows items from the survey that varied significantly from the group as a whole and showed a statistical trend toward variance in terms of placement disruption. Table 10 illustrates one item that varied significantly and 11 other items with a trend toward variance from the group as a whole on average scores for developmental disruption.

As table 9 indicates, foster mothers who reported fewer than three close friends were significantly more likely to experi-

Table 9. Number of Disrupted Placements for 21 Foster Families Who Had 29 Foster Children Participate in the Follow-Up Study

	Number of families	Disrupted placements per family	Percent
Total Samples	21	8	38.1
■ Gender preference expressed	4	3	75.0
■ Fewer than three close friends	10	6	60.05
■ Preteen or teen preferred	5	3	60.0*
■ Little time spent away from foster children	12	6	50.0
■ More than three close friends	10	1	10.0
■ Moderate time spent away from foster children	9	2	22.2
■ Single-parent family	4	1	25.0
■ Know the neighbors very well	7	2	28.6

*$p < .05$

ence disrupted placements than foster mothers who reported more than three close friends. In addition, trends toward placement disruption were present in homes where teens and preteens were preferred, where a gender preference was expressed, and where the mother spent little time away from the foster children. In contrast, less placement disruption was present in single-parent families who knew their neighbors well and families in which the foster mother spent moderate amounts of time away from the foster children.

As table 10 indicates, foster children placed with parents who expressed a gender preference demonstrated significantly less improvement in symptoms of developmental disruption. In addition, trends toward less improvement were present among foster children in homes with fewer than six family members, where an age preference was expressed, and where the foster mother spent little time away from the family. In contrast, trends toward more

Table 10. Average Initial Developmental Disruption (DD) and Improvement for 29 Children Placed in 21 Foster Homes

	Number of families	Average initial DD ratings per family	Average DD improvement per family
Total Samples	21	1.90 ± 0.22	0.68 ± 0.15
▪ Gender preference	4	1.37 ± 0.50	0.09 ± 0.22*
▪ Time away from foster children often spent with family members	10	1.65 ± 0.35	0.41 ± 0.20
▪ Age preference for preteens or teens	5	1.48 ± 0.62	0.43 ± 0.42
▪ Family size less than six	11	1.80 ± 0.32	0.47 ± 0.23
▪ Age preference for younger children	9	1.74 ± 0.31	0.54 ± 0.19
▪ Little time spent away from foster children	12	1.65 ± 0.30	0.58 ± 0.18
▪ No preference by age	6	2.27 ± 0.33	1.08 ± 0.26
▪ No gender preference	15	2.29 ± 0.19	0.98 ± 0.15
▪ Time away from foster children seldom spent with family members	11	2.12 ± 0.29	0.92 ± 0.21
▪ Family size six or more	10	2.01 ± 0.31	0.91 ± 0.18
▪ Single-parent family	4	2.27 ± 0.48	0.86 ± 0.32
▪ Moderate time spent away from foster children	9	2.23 ± 0.33	0.81 ± 0.26

*$p < .05$

improvement were present among single-parent families with more than six members, where parents expressed no preference by age or gender, and where the foster mother spent moderate amounts of time away from other family members.

We interpreted this information to indicate that therapeutic success among foster parents in our program was consistent with the personal qualities generally associated with effective psychotherapy, such as outstanding interpersonal skills, a tolerance for different types of children, and a positive sense of self. Contrary to our expectations, social network factors, such as church attendance, extended family involvement, and the use of support groups, did not correlate directly with measures of success.

Therapeutic Techniques

Over the years, it became apparent that experienced foster parents applied certain techniques tactically within the general therapeutic milieu. Portions of transcripts from interviews with three of the most effective therapeutic foster parents are presented below to illustrate the blend of approaches employed during various stages of placement.

Forming a Therapeutic Relationship. Forming a relationship and establishing treatment goals were the initial steps for therapy in placement. In the following transcript, Mrs. T, an experienced foster mother, formulates her initial approach to Rita, an abused, neglected, behaviorally disturbed girl who came to her home with an unrepaired harelip and cleft palate:

> Those first few months there was so many who told me it wouldn't work, and that it was just impossible for Rita to turn out to be a real person. But in my mind, I said it could be done, and I began to forget about myself and concentrate on Rita. Some things she did were very unbecoming. I just couldn't believe it was happening, but I still saw that it could be corrected. Rita was ten when we first saw her story in the newspaper. They were fixing to send her out of the city to a group home because there were no foster parents, and her picture was in the Sunday paper. At first I did not pay much attention to it, but the next Sunday her picture came back in the paper, and I got very interested in this little girl. Something about her attached me, and so we had meetings and meetings and finally [the caseworker] brought the picture to one of our [support group] meetings one night. I told him that I would like to try, but they thought she was kinda old for my two kids because they are just small kids, somewhere like four and six. We still did not change our minds. So we worked to get Rita for about two weeks. We visited her at [the psy-

chiatric hospital] and after about four days they arranged for her to come into our home. When I got her I wanted to know everything that was connected with her, with her physical problems and all. That was my way of putting things together. We visited Rita, viewed all of her school-work, and talked with some of the people from the psychiatric hospital.

I believe Rita's problem was connected to when she was born with a cleft palate. I believe somewhere down the line it was connected with that, and her not having a parent [who would care for her], and she just being loose from institution to institution. Well, to me it was just like [her birth family was] being a bunch of cows or hogs together, so they could get together [and molest each other] when they wanted to. So, it was pretty hard to teach her [prosocial] things, to get her away from that.

Rita was a wild one. She needed very close attention. Everything had to go her way. She fought a lot with other kids and expected you to take up for her. She liked to use weapons, knives, and so [because it was dangerous] we had to go along with her for about three weeks. At first it was something kind of like a honeymoon, just sugar and cream. But there came a day...when things got pretty rough, but we continually worked with Rita. We began to talk to her and tried to make her understand what was right, what was wrong. We began to get her interested in working with other kids. We put her in the church choir and had other kids to go around with her. By us not using alcohol beverages or bad language around home she began to fall into [a more positive] category. She did not want to do [antisocial behaviors] either....We took notes very closely on Rita. I wrote a book about that thick on her, putting one and one together, piecing it together.

It was very rough at the church when she first went there. Rita wasn't a beautiful sight. She has a cleft palate, and she wasn't very pretty. When the children first saw her they thought she was something ugly, just something to pick on, and I could see it hurting her. She was fixing to turn church out of her one day. I came out of the choir stand and sat beside her and told her there is something wrong with everybody. I said, "Look at me....there is something wrong with me," and she wanted to know what. I said, "Look at how short I am, and how stout I am." So, she began to go along with some people, and that was very beautiful, but still there was something wrong. It was worse than I thought. One day we had come from church and stopped over for ice cream at this one boy's parents' home. One of the sisters came down the stairs and said, "Rita is in the closet." So, we ran up there, and sure enough there they were [acting out sexually]. But, she looked so cut and hurt over the incident that I felt in my mind I shouldn't scold her, but that was the way I was teaching her. I began to teach her all the things that I know in my mind, every chance we had. You know, after some of the [sexually] aggressive bossy boys came around she had a change [to being more self-protective].

The Middle Stages of Therapy. Use of the therapeutic relationship for problem-solving and emotional maturation was focal during the middle stages of treatment in our program, as it is in most long-term residential treatment programs. Techniques employed by three foster families midway through therapy are illustrated below. First, Rita's foster mother describes a critical episode that occurred during the middle part of her therapy.

I had Rita for about two years, and with hard work I could see the turn. She began to want to do [positive] things. I would give the church a great big portion of [credit for] that, [particularly for] the support that I got with her after I felt the kids make fun of her. [One day], I got up and asked my pastor if I could make a speech because I wanted these parents to know that she was a little human being even though she wasn't as pretty as some and she was a little strange, but she was a human being. He gave me the permission to do that, and I got up and talked to the whole congregation. I stood her up there in front so they could see her. I had a feeling they would be on my side, and they would get behind me and push me with the girl. They began to bring her into their homes and different places. Then Rita began to grow up. That was her turning point. She felt she wasn't loved. I had to take one portion of love for the two little ones. ...I had to take [some of] my love from my husband and he had to take [some of] his love from the [other] kids and just give it to her. Well, at that point we got those two little fellows to understand that big sister had problems, and they should help her. Without [my husband] being behind me, when things were too rough for me I don't think I could have made it. I think little girls and boys always go to their daddy. He would step in and help us out, help me out.

As illustrated above, Mrs. T used individual, family, and group techniques to coax Rita toward change.

In the next transcript, Mr. & Mrs. R demonstrate a different style of therapy toward similar goals. Here they are discussing recent developments concerning Wendy, their seven-year-old foster daughter. Wendy, who had cystic fibrosis, had been in the foster home for two years at the time of the taping. Mrs. L, Wendy's biological mother, had recently reappeared after being virtually out of touch for two years. The event was upsetting the foster family, and was a potential danger to Wendy's health. During the taping, her foster parents were discussing how to help Wendy accept responsibility for the care that her illness required, and to cope with feelings of deprivation as well as fears of loss, death, and separation, including another probable loss of contact with her biological mother.

Mr. R: For the first time in two years, actually I think within the next few months, we have a real opportunity to make some inroads with the girl's mother. ...[Mrs. L] assumed that she could have no contact with the girls, and she just called to check and ask my wife, "How are the girls?"

Mrs. R: I offered her a visit. She said that she had been out of town. She had just gotten back, and had a job, didn't say where, and did not give a phone number for us to get in touch with her. So, we simply wait for her.

Mr. R: Tentatively, we've told her to visit next Sunday, and she is going to call us back and let us know if she can arrange for transportation...we have pretty well decided it should be a supervised visit. It's not so much that I'm not afraid of what Mrs. L will do. I'm afraid of what Wendy will do to Mrs. L, that she will badger her to death. The workings of Wendy's mind never fail to amaze me. Somewhere in the process of going to my mother and stepfather's home, 300 miles away [for a Thanksgiving Day visit], she just totally ignored me...and played up to my stepfather and my brother. ...We were there for four days. It was such an obvious thing. She would walk past me and not look. It was the first time that's ever happened. And as soon as we got back home [and it was] time for bed, then right away Wendy is going to give me a big hug and a kiss. So I said, "Wendy, if you can ignore me for four days, we don't need that right now," and we just let it go at that.

Mrs. R: It looked like she was mad at him, and trying to make him feel sorry for it.

Mr. R: I get the feeling that she was trying to punish me. ...Wendy isn't over it yet. She's being bused to school, and she is making so many decisions now. I had a little talk with her a week ago. It was really cold outside and she was continually pushing to go outside to play. So we sat down and I shared with her what her disease meant. These are all things she had heard before, [including] what the problem was, what would happen if she went outside, and that she could get sick. "[You] would have to go to the hospital, and could possibly even die. ...Wendy, you have got to start making that decision for yourself. If you want to go outside and play tomorrow, then you can go." I gave her the right to go. She still had to ask, "Can I go outside?" But I told her if she wanted to go outside then she could go...

At this point in the transcript, Mr. R is asked if anything had occurred within the family that increased their focus on illness or death. He responds:

Mr. R: Come to think of it, the hamster died. We discovered that within 24 hours of the time I talked to Wendy. Of course, I got a straight-pan face from her when I talked to her, but that's normal for her. She is in total control of herself, usually.

Mrs. R: She is listening. [I know] because I told the boys they had to wear scarves, even if they didn't want to. Luke was going around [saying] "I can't find mine," but Wendy said, "He could use mine." I said, "That's fine, we have enough scarves. I found the other one for Luke. That's fine. If you want to go to the hospital, you don't need to wear a scarf." She [then] wrapped the scarf around her face. She's had it around her face every day this week.

Mr. R: I've noted how she has been dressing. She had been very religious about it, putting on her scarf and taking care of herself. I guess it got to the point where she figured she had to start making the decisions on her own... Wendy has to get medicine at midnight...They [Wendy and her biological sister] are both on antibiotics, they have been for five or six weeks now. ...We have been spending a lot of money and losing sleep over this...

Mrs. R: The kids don't wake up [easily]. They keep saying, "You didn't get me up last night to take my pills."

Mr. R: They haven't remembered a midnight dosage for weeks. I've learned how to get them up, to walk out there and take the medicine and go back to bed. But Wendy will tell you the next day, "You forgot to give me my medicine."

In this case, the foster parents worked together as a team and were generally successful in their goal of helping Wendy improve her self-care toward better self-esteem. Wendy's mother did, in fact, continue to reappear and lose contact with her children periodically. The foster parents were able to help Wendy accept this reality and yet to continue to care for herself. She and her sister eventually became reattached to their father and his new wife and went to live with them, while Mr. and Mrs. R continued to provide support over time to all concerned.

The third illustration of technique during mid-therapy concerns Sharon, a nine-year-old girl who had been placed in Mrs. I's foster home three years earlier on a court order. Sharon had been molested by her stepfather, and her mother, Mrs. J, was unable to cope. The couple subsequently divorced, and

Mrs. J remarried and moved to Hawaii. She phoned Sharon frequently, but refused to accept her back. Although Sharon made an adequate, even loving, adjustment to the foster home and to school, she suffered a continuing cycle of guilt and depression, exhibiting pathology similar to her mother's.

In this transcript, Mrs. I describes her therapeutic approach to Sharon's problem.

> When [Sharon] gets angry she will lash out and say, "How would you like it if your parents hated your guts and don't want you to live with them?" I try to help her by telling her that her mother doesn't hate her, [that she] actually loves her, but she just can't cope with taking care of a child on a full-time basis. I tell her it's not her [Sharon's] fault, but she needs to hear that from her mother. Mrs. J is in Hawaii, remarried and doing well financially, but remains too self-involved to think about Sharon.

> Sharon is very excited because she won a chess tournament, a trophy in a chess tournament for being the best girl player. She was telling her mother about it on the phone, and her mother just skipped right over it as though it didn't count one way or the other. This really hurt Sharon. Sharon commented about it later, and I said, "Yes, I noticed that your mother slipped over that real quickly." Sharon asked, "How come?" I said, "I don't know. I guess she had more important things to talk to you about at that particular time than to listen [to information] about you." This was Sunday. So, Monday afternoon the phone rings and it's Mrs. J. I think, "Oh Lord, you have changed your mind and you want her to come back." No. The problem is even bigger.

> Jean asks me a lot of questions about Sandy [one of the other foster children]. She says, "Sharon and Sandy get along real well. They are kind of like family aren't they? They are more like family than anybody else. ...You know why I am asking these questions, don't you?" I say, "No, I don't," but in the back of my mind I'm thinking, "Oh, no! She wants to adopt Sandy." Mrs. J says that they might want Sandy to come to Hawaii with Sharon this summer, and spend four or five weeks, so they can get a feel for

each other. She said, "We'll have to get the social service department out here to working on it, and it will take time. What do you expect Sandy will think?" I thought fast and said, "Do you want to know the truth? Right off the top of my head, I'm going to say that Sandy will say no, but then I've been wrong before." I didn't want to give Mrs. J a low blow and send her back to the hospital. I thought I would leave a little hope for her. ...[Now] I have to compose a letter and give her my thoughts.

My letter is going to say it's not practical for her to adopt Sandy. ...Knowing Mrs. J's depression states, she may not be altogether rational. I'm going to tell her that Sandy is just getting to the point where an attachment is being made here, but she is not secure enough to be moved to another home. Sandy is never going to find out [about Mrs. J's idea] if I have anything to say about it, because then I think it would cause friction between Sandy and Sharon. And I don't need Sharon saying, "Oh, you don't love me like you do Sandy."

In this case, the foster mother expertly helped Sharon and her mother remain reality-focused, enabled them to relate better, and sensitively bolstered their self-esteem. Eventually, the mother and daughter were reunited permanently on better terms and continued a supportive relationship with the foster mother.

Completing Therapy. The final task in therapy is for the therapist to disengage, yet maintain a strong enough relationship to preserve behavioral and emotional gains. In this transcript, Mrs. T, Rita's foster mother, describes how she helped her foster child grow away from the foster home.

Rita done real well until, I don't know, I guess she hit that age. ...She got very mean, sassy, and she wanted to be on her own. I think it was all because they wouldn't work [with cosmetic surgery] on her mouth. When she was 16 she got it into her head she wanted to leave. She just had to get out. She told me one day, "Why don't you turn me loose. I know you're holding on to me. Let me go." I said, "You really want to go?" She said, "Yes." But I called the caseworker, and I found out she really didn't want to go as bad as she pretended. ...You see Rita thought if she got away from home and into the group home, that she would be able to come back here when she got ready, and continue to do the [adolescent sexual] things in her mind that she wanted to do. But when she got there, she found it was more strict than at our home, and then she began to want to come on home [saying], "I want to come home. Mom, I want to come home. I love you so much."

But I knew Rita well enough to know when she is real and when she is not. She tells me, "I'll never do this, I'll never do that." But she's now just about 18 years old [and also says] "I'm going to go when I please and come when I please."…I visit her every weekend…and think of her as my daughter…because she didn't have nobody after she went out there. I will never be able to turn her [completely] loose. We turned up quite a few of her [biological] uncles, after we spent a lot of time looking…and we know who her mother is. …We just found out that [her mother is] in the penitentiary. …We wrote her some letters. …Rita found out and wanted to find out who her mother was. …And I said, well, I said I was already working on that. …This week the caseworker and I are going to go down to the penitentiary to meet Rita's mother…and she has other family there too.

Rita disengaged from the therapeutic home and was placed in a group home. With the help of her foster mother, however, she was able to continue to focus on important personal developmental goals at the group home. Eventually, she got the needed surgery, reconciled with her foster family, and now considers them as grandparents to her own four children.

The Foster Parents' Therapeutic Role
Foster parents in this program filled a unique role. Their task was to guide disturbed foster children toward competent development and pride in their backgrounds. Appropriate techniques the foster parents applied included behavior modification, cognitive restructuring, and social skills training. The one essential element of their task, however, was always loving care. Their work was emotional and down-to-earth, yet conceptual as well. Consider the following tribute from a foster child:

To My Mom (Foster Mom)

Love is…being with you

Love is…

Love is something people feel. Some people think it's just another silly feeling, but to me it's more than another feeling.
Love to me is when a person really cares for another person, and will do his or her darndest to help the person that is in trouble, or that is in need of help.

Like this real special person in my life. She has done her darndest to keep me out of trouble and walking a straight line. Today I found out that she really cared for me. To tell you the truth I really care for her and the family.

Well, I hope she reads this little note I wrote to her and others, and hope she remembers that I really Love and Care for her.

Spell It With Capital Letters.

Remember, to keep a family together you must love one another.

REFERENCES

Bauer, J., and Heinke, W. "Treatment Family Homes for Disturbed Foster Children." *CHILD WELFARE* LV, 7 (1976): 478-489.

Carbino, R. *Foster Parenting: An Updated Review of the Literature.* New York: The Child Welfare League of America, 1980.

Hampson, R., and Tavormina, J. "Feedback from the Experts: A Study of Foster Mothers." *Social Work* 25, 2 (1981): 108-112.

Holmes, T.H., and Rahe, R.E. "The Social Readjustment Rating Scale." *Journal of Psychosomatic Research* 11, 2 (Aug. 1967): 213-218.

Paulson, M.J.; Grossman, S.; and Shapiro, G. "Child-Rearing Attitudes of Foster Home Mothers." *Journal of Community Psychology* 2, 1 (1974): 11-14.

Petersen, J.C., and Pierce, A.D. "Socioeconomic Characteristics of Foster Parents." *CHILD WELFARE* LIII, 5 (1974): 295-304.

7. SOCIAL POLICY AND THE NETWORK EFFECT

Considered from the broad perspectives of time and practice, therapeutic foster care is an affirmative and realistic residential treatment option with special relevance for contemporary child welfare services. This chapter provides a summary of our work, discusses ways in which it fits within the context of today's social services, and suggests policies that could enhance the system as a whole.

Taking Stock of Experience

Our work had much in common conceptually with the contemporary family-oriented programs that treat pathology in a community setting [Braukmann et al. 1984; Bribitzer and Verdiek 1988; Fein et al. 1990; Hess and Folaran 1991; Snodgrass and Bryant 1989]. As described in chapters 2 and 3, our approach was long-term and comprehensive, and involved the child's original family and a secondary network of helping professionals. Structurally, the foster parents facilitated normative and corrective experiences; the caseworker assumed leadership for team, network, and developmental continuity; and the child psychiatrist helped treat psychopathology within a context of total care.

Inasmuch as they had a multiplicity of psychiatric, medical, familial, and economic difficulties, the population we served over a decade ago is strikingly similar to the young survivors of AIDS, drug abuse, and violence currently challenging our public welfare system [American Public Welfare Association 1990; Diamond et al. 1990; Rendon et al. 1989; Taylor-Brown 1991]. Like the children in contemporary populations, those who participated in our program came from a variety of welfare and mental health agencies and courts, usually after having been removed from their biological families at a young age and having subsequently failed to maintain at least one foster placement. Children of color were overrepresented, medical problems

- Relationship therapy took place over time within the foster homes and was generally helpful.
- The program was most helpful for children with learning, developmental, and neuropsychiatric disorders.
- Foster parents who were most successful in the program were typically experienced, mature, skillful, well socialized, and independent.
- Enduring attachments to foster families usually increased the foster children's sense of affiliation with their biological families, enhanced positive morale, and fostered a willingness to accept support during later years.

Figure 9. Summary of Our Experience with Therapeutic Foster Care

were frequent, and psychiatric disorders, particularly conduct and anxiety disorders, predominated. Further, the parents and families our program served presented problems equal in severity to those of their children.

After 10 years of treatment and research, as detailed in chapters 4, 5, and 6, four integrative conclusions concerning the program were reached. Each conclusion is listed in figure 9 and discussed below to clarify how our experiences with therapeutic foster care may be more generally applicable.

Relationship Therapy. Our program began with the simple assumption that therapeutic foster care as residential treatment would benefit disturbed children. The program sought basically to facilitate long-term therapeutic relationships with foster parents. It was assumed that self-regulation, positive self-regard, and a sense of mastery would increase by means of emotional attachment and differentiation similar to that which has since been delineated for normal children [Emde 1985; Flannery 1987; Grossman and Grossman 1991; Luthar and Zigler 1991; Mangelsdorf et al. 1990; Stroufe 1988]. Conditions that were considered essential for relationship therapy within the program consisted of stable placements and attachments to foster parents and an atmosphere that was noncompetitive with biological families.

The behaviors used to evaluate the presence or absence of effective therapy were based on symptoms of biobehavioral dysregulation and traumatic stress associated with disrupted development [Demb 1991; Eth and Pynoos 1985; Ferholt et al. 1985; Haywitz et al. 1980; Kaufman 1991; Kiser et al. 1991; Kluft 1985; Mouridsen and Nielsen 1990; Simms 1989; Zimmerman 1988]. Stability of placements within the program, the presence or absence of emotional attachments to foster parents and biological family members, and stages of therapy were measured and surveyed separately.

Analysis of the program's results in terms of relationship therapy was affirmative. We found that the placements were adequately maintained, attachments to foster parents had occurred, therapy went through roughly predictable yearly stages, symptoms of biobehavioral dysregulation had improved, foster children who felt most attached to their foster parents had benefited the most, and relationships with biological families had not been adversely affected.

Nevertheless, there were no miracle cures. Perturbations within placements were typical, and complex problems continued. Children who improved the most tended to have entered younger, experienced more abuse and neglect, and had a greater number of foster placements than others in our program. In contrast, those who improved least tended to have histories of frequent psychiatric hospital and group home placements and were likely to be scheduled for return to a dysfunctional middle-class home. Like the authors of another recent study, we found that the emotional investment children made in foster care increased their chances for eventually attaining positive adaptations [Fanshel et al. 1990]. We thus conclude that therapeutic foster care is a reasonable residential treatment option during middle childhood for stress-related cases of moderate intensity from complex family situations.

Psychiatric Integration. Our research also found—unexpectedly—that foster children with developmental disabilities and related disorders improved more than the group as a whole. All but two of the 71 children in our study had psychiatric diagnoses, two-thirds had more than one such diagnosis, and well over half demonstrated other indications of psychiatric disorders, such as a history of hospitalization or psychotropic medication. It was therefore logical to include a child psychiatrist on the therapeutic foster care team [Kliman et al. 1982; Levin et al. 1976; Reiger 1972]. Moreover, it was striking when correlation studies indicated that the foster children had a clear need for traditional psychiatric techniques: those with neurologic, developmental, organic personality, and attention-deficit disorders tended to show more improvement than others in the program. We believe that it was the direct presence of a child psychiatrist within the program that enabled the caseworkers and foster parents to cope specifically with these difficult cases.

Learning disabilities, retardation, neurological disorders, and other serious psychiatric and medical conditions have been prevalent in surveys of foster children generally [De Fries et al. 1964; Kavaler and Swire 1983; Moffat et al. 1985; Schor 1982]. Nevertheless, most contemporary therapeutic foster care programs have not incorporated a psychiatrist into their treatment teams [Foster Family Based Treatment Association 1991; Meadowcroft and Trout 1991].

In view of the considerable progress in child psychiatry that has taken place during the decade since our program ended, it seems time again to apply psychiatric techniques and findings in community settings. This is a suggestion that assumes increased importance when one considers the special needs of young children from dysfunctional families with substance abuse problems, who are neurologically involved, behaviorally disturbed, and continue to swell the caseloads of child protection agencies.

Competent Parenting. The tasks undertaken by the foster parents in our program, described in chapter 3, entailed considerable skill and independent judgment. They had to maintain families, parent children, engage in relationship therapy, comfort their foster children's biological families, and deal with school systems, social agencies, and psychiatric and other medical resources. Those who exemplified our program were usually middle-aged, middle- or low-income, and well established. In this way, they were similar to foster parents in other therapeutic programs [Goldston 1982;

Snodgrass and Bryant 1989]. The particular mix in our group involved single and married parents from a variety of ethnic backgrounds. Their traditional source of support was friends and extended family, an orientation that translated easily into reliance on the program's therapeutic team and support networks. As individuals, they were realistic, accessible, persistent, skillful, socially competent, independent, and caring. As a group, they tended to be active in churches. Their primary motivation for fostering was ideological and unusually altruistic. They belonged to well-functioning family and social networks, and possessed a tough-minded dedication to the welfare of their families.

Results from our follow-up study indicate that the foster parents who were most successful in our particular set of circumstances were unusually nonpossessive and self-aware, and exhibited professionalism in relation to their work with the children. Because they were so independent, even the most competent foster parents were sometimes misperceived as oppositional. They were opposed to authority not on principle, but only when they had an honest difference of opinion on matters they considered vital to their families. After years of working with these foster parents, the impression emerged of exceptionally competent, mature, loving, experienced, well-socialized people who made a vocation of child-rearing and family life.

We were able to attract resourceful individuals with genuine motivation, skill, and autonomy to our program by recruiting widely with positive advertising and then openly presenting the genuine difficulties of the task at hand, thus enabling them to gradually drop out or to participate in the program. Once they had received training, were licensed, and had accepted children for therapeutic foster care, however, they were unambivalently supported. A similar process of autonomous participation of foster parents has been described in a more recent program [Gross and Campbell 1991], and could be central to the wider recruitment of autonomous foster families. We have come to believe that recruiting and clearly supporting well-motivated and loving individuals are fundamental to success in any type of out-of-home care.

Outstanding foster and adoptive parents are skilled individuals who choose to care for other people's children. Although their work transcends economics, it represents a vital resource for civilized care and is particularly important for portions of the community that are socially and economically distressed.

The Network Effect. A unique advantage of therapeutic foster care as residential treatment is its potential to help disturbed children through community networks that may endure throughout their lives. This element of the program assumed particular importance over time, since mental health, family, and school problems tended to persist beyond initial expectations and sometimes became chronic as the children we treated grew to adolescence.

We found that enduring attachments between foster parents and their current or former foster children seemed to increase the likelihood that the children would maintain networks of beneficial relationships at school, with helping professionals, and elsewhere in the community throughout and beyond adolescence. Adolescents who had maintained such relationships at the time of the follow-up study were more likely than others to demonstrate positive adaptation, positive morale, acceptance of help when needed, and a sense of belonging. Moreover, we found that other members of the foster children's biological families also utilized their children's networks.

Chronic and serious problems will probably always exist within society and among its children. Formal programs tend to be transient, but personal relationships, such as those that formed between foster parents and children in our program, have a chance to endure. It seems, after all, that thoughtful effort can bring people together in helpful, relatively permanent ways, and that caring for others within society has intrinsic value.

Comprehensive Services for Disturbed Children

Throughout our work with therapeutic foster care, it was apparent that treatment was most successful when it occurred within a system of balanced services that was supported by realistic social policies. Three planning factors proved particularly important: the skills of the clinical team, the intensity of their services, and the availability of related services. We realize that system planning and social policy are determined most directly by the financial and political variables discussed in chapter 1. Yet we also believe that adequate attention to contextual variables keeps plans and policies consistent with the biological, psychological, and social realities of clinical problems that the programs are meant to alleviate.

Foster Care in Context. Table 11 schematically presents therapeutic foster care within a context of related programs. Examples of programs that emphasize parenting, educational or social services, and mental health skills are listed by category according to their approximate order of technical intensity. A fourth category illustrates programs in which professional skills are combined in relatively equal proportions. Each program listed requires proficiency and dedication. Those that are more intensive, however, are also usually more structured, more expensive, less familiar to the public and, therefore, harder to support. All are vehicles for therapeutic options within a comprehensive system, and for the best effect, are to be applied in a complementary rather than a competitive fashion.

Examples of programs that emphasize parenting and interface with therapeutic foster care include baby-sitting, day care, comprehensive parenting for normal children, respite care, parenting adoptive children, foster parenting, and parenting children with special needs or terminally ill children. Examples of programs where educational or social services predominate range from income maintenance and routine family support to special education and the services of crisis centers and residential schools. Programs that primarily emphasize mental health techniques include self-help groups, simple behavioral therapy, special outpatient services for child protection [Molin 1988], support groups for foster parents [Steinhauer et al. 1989], special services for adopted children [Herson 1990], outpatient clinics for children with severe psychopathology who require pharmacotherapy or intensive psychotherapy, day programs, group homes, and acute psychiatric hospitals.

95

Programs for therapeutic foster care are usually built around a mixture of skills. Some focus primarily on social work, with secondary parenting and mental health services obtained only when necessary [Woolf 1990]. In contrast, therapeutic foster care, as exemplified by our experience, combined the various professions in more or less equal proportions, with specialized parenting, social work, and educational or mental health techniques all becoming primary at one time or another, depending on individual circumstances and needs. The fact that our program emphasized cooperation among skilled components enabled us to tailor and time services according to case requirements and to interact with a broad array of other resources as necessary. Thus, children and families could leave and return to the program with minimal loss of relationship or therapeutic continuity.

Other programs for child care combine core skills at various levels of intensity with a synergism similar to that of therapeutic foster care programs. Some are conducted with relatively low intensity, such as parent education; some with medium intensity, such as outpatient child guidance; and others with high intensity, such as residential treatment. One particular type of program combines family therapy and parent education with social, educational, and mental health services in an effort to preserve or reunify families [Cimmarusti 1992; Hess et al. 1992; Pecora et al. 1992]. Such family preservation efforts are typically close to the community, sensitive to cultural differences, and developmentally focused. They are usually less intensive than ongoing therapeutic foster care, but may include or collaborate with therapeutic foster care programs.

Like other multifaceted community-based programs, therapeutic foster care is a helpful anchor for comprehensive services, but requires programmatic validity, diagnostic clarity, specificity of indications, consistent application, open communications, and the willingness to cooperate with other service programs. It remains a challenge for society to facilitate networks of services for children whose complex problems mandate comprehensive care.

Table 11. Comprehensive Services for Children

	Therapeutic Foster Care within a Continuum of Technical Skills			
Technical Intensity	Parenting	Educational and Social Services	Mental Health Services	Combined Programs
Low	▪ Baby-sitting	▪ Income Maintenance	▪ Self-Help Programs	▪ Parent Education
Moderate	▪ Day Care ▪ Respite Care	▪ Routine Family Support	▪ Behavioral Programs	▪ Child Guidance Centers
High	▪ Comprehensive Parenting ▪ Adoptive Parenting ▪ Foster Parenting • For Children with Special Needs • For Terminally Ill Children	▪ Child Protective Investigations ▪ Public Schooling ▪ Special Education ▪ Crisis Placements ▪ Specialized Foster Care ▪ Training Schools	▪ Professional Outpatient Services ▪ Day Hospitals ▪ Group Homes ▪ Acute Psychiatric Hospitalization	▪ Family Preservation Services ▪ Drug/Alcohol Programs ▪ Therapeutic Foster Care ● Residential Treatment

Policy Considerations. Services for children and families encompass sensitive issues involving multiple aspects of public policy [Fine 1985]. Our program was directly influenced by public policy because it served a variety of extreme medical, educational, family, and therapeutic needs. It required consistent public support because behaviors among the children and families it served tended to be extreme. Elements of policy support that were and remain basic to our and other therapeutic networks, as listed in figure 10, include an informed public, positive legislation, administrative clarity, judicial restraint, and a base of pertinent technical skills and knowledge.

Public Awareness. Over the years we came to believe that adequate care within our program depended on how well the public acknowledged the condition of the children and families they expected us to help. The public, however, was not well informed at that time, nor is it now. Negative and dramatic foster care situations receive publicity at the expense of stable and positive programs, and the excellent work of model foster families is less than universally appreciated. Average citizens deplore child abuse, demand child protection, and favor child-rearing within the biological family. Yet the public appears to recoil from the harsh realities of abuse and family incompetence and the consequent requirement for long-term and relatively expensive solutions. Paradoxically, family foster care placement has sometimes been viewed as a cause of social problems, with condemnation directed at families whose core motivation is to help.

The main issue to be placed before society is how well we can help children develop and families function, yet reducing the prevalence of child abuse and the number of children in foster care is usually more widely discussed. Prevention is certainly necessary and desirable, and presents a measure of success toward broader goals, but fundamental changes in public attitude may depend on our ability to publicize model programs involving exemplary foster families. Efforts to identify, empower, and reward exceptional parents in each community contribute to this goal.

Creating broad networks of support for the ever-larger numbers of children raised in undersupported, overstressed, sin-

---

- A positively informed public
- Legislation to enable care
- Administrative clarity
- Judicial restraint
- A base of relevant skills and knowledge

Figure 10. Policy Aspects of Cooperative Parenting

gle-parent families is expected to be a major public issue into the next century [Edelman 1987], and children of color will remain particularly in need [NBCDI 1989]. Our work and that of others has established that relatively successful approaches to the complex problems of out-of-home care are possible, but require consistency over the long run [Fein 1991; Kates et al. 1991].

Legislation. Federal support for families has been a recent topic for Congressional committees and nonpartisan private commissions. Generally, their recommendations include measures to guarantee income security, facilitate educational achievement, prepare adolescents for adult life, strengthen and support families, protect vulnerable children, create a moral climate for child rearing, and provide adequate health care [Jacobs and Davies 1991].

At the federal level, legislation specific to foster care emphasizes systems that identify and teach children in government-supported foster placements, encourage biological family reunification, and promote adoption when reunification is not possible. Additional measures would provide access to specialized preschool, educational, and mental health services for foster children with problems [Allen 1991].

State and local legislation related to foster care is more likely to be concerned with regulation than national legislation, and more likely to be influenced by local conditions. In most states, it focuses on licensing foster homes, training foster parents, keeping track of children who are placed, preserving reunited biological families, and adoption. Other state laws affect foster homes less directly. These laws include measures that place minors in out-of-home care as a consequence of status or index offenses, for help with disabilities, for protection, or because of parental death, disability, or incarceration. Other laws allocate funds for education and medical and mental health care, and ensure that civil and criminal measures are taken against child abuse and neglect.

In our experience, state laws exert a more profound influence on children in foster care than federal measures do, but the effects of these various laws on children in placement are sometimes contradictory or confusing. For example, it is not unusual for children to be placed away from their biological families because of serious abuse, but later reunited without protection on the grounds of family preservation. Worse still, some are removed from secure placements only because procedural requirements or licensing laws have changed. Further, psychiatric hospitalization is often more readily available than less expensive partial care alternatives because of the way in which legislation distributes funds. As a result, hospitalization is sometimes used even when not strictly indicated.

In state and local laws, the outcomes for children who are placed away from home would probably be improved by a clearer focus on developmental and therapeutic continuity in foster care; better financial, legal, and emotional protection for foster families; improved service delivery based on the comprehensive needs of each child; and stronger administrative structures to support networks for ongoing care.

Administrative Clarity. Clarity in the administration of resources, context, and timing is also essential for constructive out-of-home care. In principle, every placement should enhance personal abilities, family ties, and community resources. In actuality, feelings of vulnerability are a predictable human response when children are taken away from their loved ones. Under these circumstances, even minor or transient lapses in administrative support may create an extraordinary and self-reinforcing atmosphere of anxiety and helplessness for the children, their families, foster parents, and others who try to improve the situation. As a consequence, regulatory, budgetary, and personnel actions that are ill considered on an administrative level can be profoundly disruptive on a clinical level.

Administratively, out-of-home care is a heterogeneous task. Placements vary in age group, from infancy to adolescence; in sponsorship, from state-sponsored to informal arrangements with relatives; in venue, from departments of social service to the criminal justice system; in goals, from custodial to therapeutic; and in kinship, from biological family members to strangers. Some placements are voluntary and others coercive; some involve large foster families and some small families; some foster parents are inexperienced and others are professional; and some placements are made in homes where there are many foster and day care children, and some in homes where there are none. Finally, networks that serve these children vary from protected preadoptive arrangements to elaborate wraparound services designed to envelop them with biological and foster relationships.

Coordination among state agencies for social, juvenile justice, education, and mental health services is particularly important. In practice, we have found that funds tend to be administered along agency lines rather than in a case-oriented fashion, and seldom address individual needs over time. For example, services for a single multiproblem family may be funded by several agencies, each of which is unaware of or uninterested in the others, and all of which are sensitive to periodic elections and annual budgets. Consequently, expensive programs may be used in given cases rather than less costly and more rational need-related programs merely because there is no mechanism to fund a needed service—as when psychiatric hospitals are not supplemented by less intensive options. Therapeutic foster care in our comprehensive program cost one-tenth as much as hospital care, and partial care programs cost even less. Yet inpatient hospitalization is consistently funded by public and private insurance, while less expensive programs are not.

Attempts to streamline administration for the population our program served were seldom lasting. Foster care review boards created to protect children in the system lacked adequate power to allocate funds, facilitate placements, or track children consistently over the years. In consequence, they tended to overemphasize presumably clear-cut issues such as adoption, control of abuse in foster homes, and reunification of children with their biological families, but were ineffective when faced with the ambiguous situations so frequent in practice. Advocacy groups that were established to remedy administrative problems also tended toward global agendas, and sometimes limited their effectiveness by becoming adversarial with service providers.

Although it is difficult to conceptualize a stable administrative arrangement capable of providing consistent services to the unstable population that uses family foster care, we believe that a long-term solution may be found through state or regional trust funds headed by nonpartisan governing boards. Public institutions of this type would be able to draw from a consistent base of private and government resources, remain relatively insulated from the profit motive and politics, and thus provide stable support.

Regardless of how society eventually chooses to fund services for vulnerable children and families, experience suggests that the intimate conduct of personal lives is best managed by the families themselves, and should remain as free as possible from the intricacies of large-scale administration. On a day-to-day basis, adequate out-of-home care depends on a multitude of small, local, case-oriented administrative decisions. These decisions involve recruiting and maintaining the best foster families, setting up thoughtful requirements for training and licensing them, and carefully matching foster children to foster families, as well as open communication, mutual respect, wisdom to make correct decisions, and courage to follow them through. Supportive administration requires the ability to reconcile freedom for intimate parenting in the foster home with orderly procedures and professional discipline.

Judicial Restraint. Legal systems also exert a powerful influence on children in foster care and their families. Courts routinely determine when children are to be formally protected, removed from or returned to their families, adopted, or made to undergo a change of custody. In many instances the court's role is even more pervasive. Visits with children in placement may be regulated, poorly coping patients may be ordered to participate in therapy or rehabilitation, and criminal proceedings may be initiated in instances of serious abuse. Children themselves may be prosecuted or placed under court supervision for status or criminal offenses.

Participation by the legal system in foster care is necessary to protect the personal rights of parents, children, and foster families. Nevertheless, from the perspective of actual practice, legal procedures present serious challenges to therapeutic care and its networks. Problems arise because of basic differences between legal and developmental processes. Legal proceedings are designed to resolve disputes over power relationships by formal processes conducted in an adult and adversarial manner with concern for confidentiality and other individual privileges. In contrast, therapeutic networks for children in out-of-home care are designed to emphasize developmental patterns, open communication, gradual decisions, and tolerance for minor deviations in an atmosphere that is comfortable for children. Restraint on the part of the legal profession is required in this context, since decisions by a court almost always take precedence over the less clearly expressed developmental and clinical needs of children and families. The exercise of such restraint may avoid disruptive or poorly timed events in the lives of children.

Situations that called for judicial restraint were numerous during our years of work with foster children. For example, "blood" or genetic relationships were honored rigidly in determining custody, and children were turned over to unknown or incompetent relatives at the expense of important emotional attachments. On various other occasions, we saw children come and go from families whose disruptive patterns resisted improvement, yet defied clear judicial resolution. Sometimes it appeared that the unrelated pressures of crowded court calendars dictated life-shaping decisions, or that judges would unrealistically attempt to micromanage cases from the bench. Occasionally, the innocence of childhood was shattered by an enforced separation from a loved parent or return to a hated one. Case managers felt intimidated when courts intervened and hindered their use of independent judgment. Psychiatric and other mental health evaluations and hospitalizations were sometimes requested in such situations to balance the power of the court or provide quick solutions to complex situations in which the children could not cope.

Capable foster parents could have provided valuable insights in complex cases, and the court or guardian ad litem could have consulted with them regarding a child's best interests, but their expertise was not widely appreciated and they experienced little protection under the law. On more than one occasion, we saw otherwise competent foster parents lose both their licenses and their foster children when they contested a court decision for the sake of their children on grounds of conscience. In so doing, they even risked having their biological children removed. Conditions of this sort lack the true measure of judicial utility and are unconnected with the pressing social needs of children and their families. For a better future, it is hoped that a way can be found to incorporate the inevitable legalities into simple, developmentally valid systems of care.

Relevant Skills and Knowledge: The Academics of Care. Education and training for core professionals within the foster care system are essential elements of policy concern. Experience suggests that certain skilled foster parents possess knowledge and techniques that could be systematized and taught, not only to other foster parents but at schools of social work, psychology, education, medicine, and law.

Out-of-home care education requires that each core profession understand the essential function of the others. Curriculum in this regard can include information about culture, kinship, and ethnicity; child development and family studies; risk factors inherent in social, family, and personal disruption; social systems; the epidemiology of medical and mental disorders; therapeutic parenting and a broad array of other mental health techniques; residential treatment; networks of support; legalities; and findings from relevant research.

Conclusion

Therapeutic foster care applies the strength of ordinary families to the challenges of extraordinary problems. Coherent care for extremely vulnerable children and families provides vital backup and essential support within our society. And a case can be made for the idea that more inclusive education, training, and research concerning the biological, psychological, and social factors that impinge on out-of-home care might counterbalance current trends toward a social system of child care with two tiers: one for the rich and one for the poor.

It seems evident in the age of technology that conscious application of timeless truths concerning parenting and human development has become essential for civilized living. Our experience with therapeutic foster care reaffirmed the basic importance of personal relationships. Individuals in the cycle of generations benefit from well-timed interconnections of joy, relaxation, and discipline, and even the youngest child interacts with other members of society as a contributing family member. Helping abused, hurt, disabled, aggressive, and even callous children and providing comfort to their families is a difficult proposition. In good hands, however, it enlarges the humane network of loving care for all concerned.

REFERENCES

Allen, M. "Crafting a Federal Legislative Framework for Child Welfare Reform." *American Journal of Orthopsychiatry* 6, 4 (1991): 610–623.

American Public Welfare Association. "Children of Substance Abusing/Alcoholic Parents Referred to the Public Welfare System: Summary of Statistical Data Obtained from States." Washington, DC: American Enterprise Institute, 1990, 61.

Braukmann, C.J.; Ramp, K.K.; Tigner, D.M.; and Wolf, M.M. "The Teaching-Family Approach to Training Group Home Parents:

Training Procedures, Validation Research, and Outcome Findings." In *Parent Training: Foundations of Research and Practice,* edited by R.F. Dangel and R.A. Polster. New York: Guilford Press, 1984.

Bribitzer, M., and Verdiek, M.J. "Home Based Family Centered Intervention: Evaluation of a Foster Care Prevention Program." *CHILD WELFARE* LXVII, 3 (1988): 255-266.

Cimmarusti, Rocco A. "Family Preservation Practice Based upon a Multisystems Approach." *CHILD WELFARE* LXXI, 3 (1992): 241-256.

De Fries, Z.; Jenkins, S.; and Williams, E.C. "Treatment of Disturbed Children in Foster Care." *American Journal of Orthopsychiatry* 34, (1964): 615-624.

Demb, J. "Reported Hyperphagia in Foster Children." *Child Abuse and Neglect* 15 (1991): 77-88.

Diamond, G.; Gurdin, P.; Wiznia, A.; Belman, A.L.; Rubenstein, A.; and Cohen, H.J. "Effects of Congenital HIV Infection on Neurodevelopmental Status of Babies in Foster Care." *Developmental Medicine and Child Neurology* 32, 11 (Nov. 1990): 999-1004.

Edelman, M.W. *Families in Peril: An Agenda for Social Change.* Cambridge, MA: Harvard University Press, 1987.

Emde, R.N. "The Affect Self: Continuities and Transformations from Infancy." In *Frontiers of Infant Psychiatry,* vol. 2, edited by J. Call, E. Galenson and R. Stimston. New York: Basic Books, 1985.

Eth, S., and Pynoos, R.S. *Post-Traumatic Stress Disorder in Children.* Washington, DC: American Psychiatric Press, 1985.

Fanshel, D.; Finch, S.J.; and Gundy, J.F. Foster *Children in Life Perspective*. New York: Columbia University Press, 1990.

Fein, E. "Issues in Foster Family Care; Where Do We Stand?" *American Journal of Orthopsychiatry* 6, 4 (1991): 578-583.

Fein, E.; Maluccio, A.N.; and Kluger, M. *No More Partings: An Examination of Foster Family Care*. Washington, DC: Child Welfare League of America, 1990.

Ferholt, J.B.; Rotnem, D.L.; Genel, M.; Leonard, M.; Carey, M.; and Hunter, D.E. "A Psychodynamic Study of Psychosomatic Dwarfism: A Syndrome of Depression, Personality Disorder, and Impaired Growth." *Journal of the American Academy of Child Psychiatry* 24, (Sept. 17, 1985): 49-57.

Fine, P. "Clinical Aspects of Foster Care." In *Foster Care: Current Issues, Policies, and Practices,* edited by J.J. Cox & R.D. Cox. Norwood, NJ: Ablex Publishing Corp., 1985.

Flannery, R.B. "From Victim to Survivor: A Stress Management Approach to the Treatment of Learned Helplessness." In *Psychological Trauma,* edited by Bessel Vander Kolk. Washington, DC: American Psychiatric Press, 1987: 217-232.

Foster Family Based Treatment Association (FFBTA). *Program Standards for Treatment Foster Care*. Minneapolis, MN: FFBTA, 1991.

Goldston, J. "The Foster Parents." In *Preventive Mental Health Services for Children Entering Foster Home Care,* edited by J.W. Kliman, W.K. Gilbert, M.H. Shaffer, and M.J. Friedman. White Plains, NY: Center for Preventive Psychiatry, 1982.

Gross, Nancy, and Campbell, Pat. "Recruiting and Selecting Treatment Parents." In *Troubled Youth in Treatment Homes: A*

Handbook of Therapeutic Foster Care. Washington, DC: Child Welfare League of America, 1990: 33-50.

Grossman, K., and Grossman, K. "Attachment Quality as an Organizer of Emotional and Behavioral Responses." In *Attachment Across the Life Cycle*, edited by P. Harris, J. Stevenson-Hinde, and C. Parkes. New York: Routledge, 1991: 93-114.

Haywitz, S.E.; Cohen, D.J.; and Shaywitz, B.A. "Behavior and Learning Difficulties in Children of Normal Intelligence Born to Alcoholic Mothers." *Journal of Pediatrics* 96 (Apr.–June 1980): 978-982.

Herson, L. "Aspects of Adoption." *Journal of Child Psychiatry and Psychology* 31, 4 (Aug. 1990): 493-510.

Hess, P.M., and Folaron, G. "Ambivalences: A Challenge to Permanency for Children." *CHILD WELFARE* LXX, 4 (1991): 403-424.

Hess, P.; Mintun, G.; Moelhman, A.; and Pitts, G. "The Family Connection Center: An Innovative Visiting Program." *CHILD WELFARE* LXXI, 1 (1992): 77-88.

Jacobs, F.H., and Davies, M.W. "Rhetoric or Reality? Child and Family Policy in the United States." *Social Policy Report* (Society for Research in Child Development) 5, 4 (1991): 1-25.

Kates, W.; Johnson, R.; Rader, M.; and Streider, F. "Whose Child Is This? Assessment and Treatment of Children in Foster Care." *American Journal of Orthopsychiatry* 6, 4 (1991): 584-591.

Kaufman, J. "Depressive Disorders in Maltreated Children." *Journal of the American Academy of Child and Adolescent Psychiatry* 30, 2 (1991): 257-265.

Kavaler, F., and Swire, M.R. *Foster Child Health Care.* Lexington, MA: Lexington Books, 1983.

Kelley, S.T., Walsh, J.H., and Thompson, K. "Birth Outcomes, Health Problems, and Neglect with Prenatal Exposure to Cocaine." *Pediatric Nursing* 17, 2 (1991): 130-136.

Kiser, L.; Heston, J.; Millsap, P.; and Pruit, D. "Physical and Sexual Abuse in Childhood: Relationship with Post-Traumatic Stress Disorder." *Journal of the American Academy of Child and Adolescent Psychiatry* 30, 5 (1991): 776-782.

Kliman, G.W.; Schaeffer, M.H.; and Friedman, M. *Preventive Mental Health Services for Children Entering Foster Home Care.* White Plains NY: Center for Preventive Psychiatry, 1982.

Kluft, R. *Childhood Antecedents of Multiple Personality Disorder.* Washington, DC: American Psychiatric Press, 1985.

Levin, S.; Rubenstein, J.S.; and Streiner, D.L. "The Parent Therapist Program: An Innovative Approach to Treating Emotionally Disturbed Children." *Hospital and Community Psychiatry* 27, 6 (June 1976): 407-410.

Luthar, S., and Zigler, E. "Vulnerability and Competence: A Review of Research on Resilience in Childhood." *American Journal of Orthopsychiatry* 6, 1 (1991): 6-22.

Mangelsdorf, S.; Gunnar, M.; Kestenbaum, R.; Lang, S.; and Andreas, D. "Infant Proneness-to-Distress Temperament, Maternal Personality and Mother-Infant Attachment: Associations and Goodness of Fit." *Child Development* 61, 3 (June 1990): 820-831.

Meadowcroft, P., and Trout, B. *Troubled Youth in Treatment Homes: A Handbook of Therapeutic Foster Care.* Washington, DC: Child Welfare League of America, 1991.

Moffatt, M.; Peddie, M.; Stulginskas, J.; Pless, B.; and Stein-metz, N. "Health Care Delivery to Foster Children: A Study." *Health and Social Work* 10, 2 (Spring 1985): 129-137.

Molin, Ronald. "Treatment of Children in Foster Care: Issues of Collaboration." *Child Abuse and Neglect* 12 (1988): 241-249.

Mouridsen, S., and Nielsen, S. "Reversible Somatotropin Deficiency Presenting as Conduct Disorder and Growth Hormone Deficiency." *Developmental Medicine and Child Neurology* 32, 12 (Dec. 1990): 1093-1098.

National Black Child Development Institute (NBCDI). *Who Will Care When Parents Can't: A Study of Black Children in Foster Care.* Washington, DC: NBCDI, 1989.

Pecora, P.J.; Fraser, M.W.; and Haapala, D.A. "Intensive Home-Based Family Preservation Services: An Update From the FIT Project." *CHILD WELFARE* LXXI, 2 (1992): 177-188.

Reiger, N.R. "Changing Concepts in Treating Children in a State Mental Hospital." *International Journal of Child Psychotherapy* 1, 4 (1972): 89-116.

Rendon, M.; Gurdin, P.; Bass, J.; and Weston, M. "Foster Care for Children with AIDS: A Psychosocial Perspective." *Child Psychiatry and Human Development* 19, 4 (1989): 256-259.

Schor, E.L. "The Foster Care System and the Health Status of Foster Children." *Pediatrics* 69, 5 (1982): 521-528.

Simms, M.D. "The Foster Care Clinic: A Community Program to Identify Treatment Needs of Children in Foster Care." *Developmental and Behavioral Pediatrics* 10, 3 (June 1989): 121-128.

Snodgrass, R.D., and Bryant, B. "Therapeutic Foster Care: A National Program Study." In *Therapeutic Foster Care: Critical*

Issues, edited by Hawkins and Breiling. Washington, DC: Child Welfare League of America, 1989.

Steinhauer, P.D.; Johnston, M.; Hornick, J.P.; Barker, P.; Snowden, M.; Santa-Barbara, J.; and Kane, B.A. "The Foster Care Research Project: Clinical Impressions." *American Journal of Orthopsychiatry* 59, 3 (July 1989): 430-441.

Stroufe, L.A. "The Role of Infant-Caregiver Attachment in Development." In *Clinical Implications of Attachment,* edited by J. Belsky and T. Nezworski. Hillsdale, NJ: Erlbaum, 1988.

Taylor-Brown, S. "The Impact of AIDS on Foster Care: A Family Centered Approach to Services in the United States." *CHILD WELFARE* LXX, 2 (1991): 193-209.

Woolf, G.A.D. "An Outlook for Foster Care in the United States." *CHILD WELFARE* LXIX, 1 (1990): 75-81.

Zimmerman, R. "Childhood Depression: New Theoretical Formulations and Implications for Foster Care Service." *CHILD WELFARE* LXVII, 1 (1988): 37-47.

ABOUT THE AUTHOR

Paul Fine, M.D., is Professor and Division Director of Child and Adolescent Psychiatry at Creighton University in Omaha, Nebraska. In both teaching and practice, Dr. Fine has emphasized the need to serve society's most vulnerable children and their families. As the author of numerous books and articles, he has influenced a generation through his innovative, effective approach to foster care.